Guide to Rapid Revision Workbook

Guide to Rapid Revision Workbook

Fourth Edition

Daniel D. Pearlman
University of Rhode Island

Allyn and Bacon
Boston • London • Toronto • Sydney • Tokyo • Singapore

Preface

The First Edition of the *Guide to Rapid Revision Workbook* grew out of a need expressed by writing instructors using the *Guide to Rapid Revision.* These instructors required exercises that would reinforce the instruction found in the parent text. But once the *Guide to Rapid Revision Workbook* was published, professors teaching writing courses from freshman composition to magazine editing began adopting the *Workbook* whether they used the parent text or not. Users of the *Workbook* attribute this wide appeal to the text's content and organization, the main features of which I have retained in this Fourth Edition.

The major features of the **Guide to Rapid Revision Workbook** *include:*

1. *An alphabetical organization:* The sections are arranged alphabetically by writing problem ("Agreement," "Comma," "Dangling Modifier," and so on), exactly as in the parent text. Both instructors and students thus gain instant access to material directly relevant to the writing problem that concerns them at the moment.

2. *How-to headnotes:* Brief, clear headnotes provide all the information and advice students need to solve the exercises on their own.

3. *A focus on frequent writing problems:* The exercises provide practice in most of the fifty areas covered by the *Guide to Rapid Revision.* The more recurrent writing errors, such as those dealt with in "Comma" and "Fragmentary Sentence," for example, are given a greater share of exercise space to provide the student with more practice with these problems.

4. *An emphasis on generative exercises:* In recognition of the process of skills development, the exercises in the *Workbook* move from the basic to the more complex—from exercises in identification and revision to those involving generation. A key feature that distinguishes this *Workbook* from others is its emphasis on generative exercises involving sentence combining and pattern practice. Extra pages are provided at the back of the *Workbook* for students to work out generative exercises. Another key feature is the deliberate choice of exercise material with a high level of interest for college students. Many of the exercises focus on lively issues in the humanities, the social sciences, and the physical sciences.

5. *Use as a self-study guide:* The answers to half of all the exercises are provided at the end of the book. The exercises for which answers are provided are marked by a large black dot: ● This self-study feature enables students to check their progress independently.

6. *Review exercises:* The instructor who wishes to give occasional quizzes will find not only that half of the exercises do not have answers in the Workbook, but also that sets of cumulative review exercises—useful for testing—are provided at the back of the text. In addition, a separate answer key for instructors is provided for all exercises.

7. *Guide to Rapid Revision Workbook* is a compact and economical workbook. This one brief, inexpensive text focuses on the points of greatest technical difficulty for the college-level writer.

Contents

Review Exercises

Answer Key

Guide to Rapid Revision
Workbook

ADJECTIVE————————————————adj

PREDICATE ADJECTIVES

An adjective modifies (describes) a noun or pronoun. Usually, an adjective occurs right next to the word it modifies: the *delicious* coffee. But sometimes the adjective is separated from the word it modifies by a verb, called a **linking verb.** The most common linking verbs are forms of *to be,* such as *is, are, was,* and the following verbs of the five senses: *sound, smell, look, feel, taste.* In the sentence, "The coffee smells *delicious,*" the adjective *delicious* modifies the noun *coffee.* The verb *smells* is a linking verb because it "links" the distant adjective *delicious* to the noun *coffee.* Adjectives that come after a linking verb are called **predicate adjectives.**

One common writing error that students make is placing an adverb—instead of an adjective—after a linking verb: "The coffee smells *deliciously.*" Use an adjective after these verbs.

> WRONG: Her makeup looked *well* on her.
> RIGHT: Her makeup looked *good* on her.
> WRONG: The wounded animal's wail sounded *horribly* in the night.
> RIGHT: The wounded animal's wail sounded *horrible* in the night.
> WRONG: My roommate felt *badly* about his recent grades.
> RIGHT: My roommate felt *bad* about his recent grades.

Feel (Look) Good Versus Feel (Look) Well

Ordinarily, *well* is an adverb. Use *well* as an adjective—after *feel, look,* etc.—only when you mean the opposite of *ill.* It is no compliment to tell a friend that she looks *well* today unless she has just recovered from an illness. If you simply mean that you admire her clothing or makeup, tell her that she looks *good.*

CORRECT FORMS OF ADJECTIVES

1. *Comparative Degree:* The comparative degree of an adjective is used when you compare two things. The comparative is usually formed by adding *-er* to adjectives of one syllable (great*er,* proud*er*) and by placing the word *more* in front of adjectives of more than one syllable (*more* useful, *more* salable). Exception: Two-syllable adjectives ending in *-y* may also add *-er: lazier* or *more lazy, angrier* or *more angry, lovelier* or *more lovely.*

2. *Superlative Degree:* The superlative degree of an adjective is used when you compare more than two things. Form the superlative by adding *-est* to the end of a one-syllable adjective (great*est,* proud*est*) and by placing the word *most* in front of adjectives of more than one syllable (*most* beautiful, *most* useful). Exception: Two-syllable adjectives ending in *-y* may also add *-est: laziest* or *most lazy,* etc.

3. *Irregular Forms:* The comparative and superlative forms of some adjectives are irregular. Good becomes *better* (comparative) and *best* (superlative); *bad* becomes *worse* and *worst.* The following examples illustrate the point:

Mary is a *good* swimmer. (No comparison here.)
Mary is a *better* swimmer than Iris. (Comparison between two.)
Mary is the *best* swimmer in the school. (Comparison among more than two.)

1

NOTE: Do not form the comparative or superlative twice:

WRONG: Arnold is a far *more better* student than Ted.
RIGHT: Arnold is a far *better* student than Ted.
WRONG: This course is *worser* than my others.
RIGHT: This course is *worse* than my others.

● Using Adjectives Appropriately

In the following sentences, circle the errors involving the misuse of adjectives. Write the proper form in the space provided. If a sentence is correct as it stands, write "C" in the blank.

EXAMPLE: __stronger__ Julie's course in assertiveness training has given her a much (more stronger) personality now than she ever had before.

___terribly___ 1. I feel terribly about predictions of worldwide disaster.

___worst___ 2. Some of the baddest predictions concern world population growth.

___good___ 3. If we take many forecasts seriously, the future does not look well for humanity.

___farther___ 4. Through computer simulations, we can "see" more farther than ever into the future.

___C___ 5. Just how bad does the computer picture look?

___well___ 6. Fewer of us seem destined to be eating as good as now.

___bad___ 7. The problem is not that the food will taste badly.

_____ 8. What sounds more disturbingly is the predicted shortage of food.

_____ 9. Is our present technology well enough to supply the world's rapidly expanding need for food?

_____ 10. Maybe future computers will predict a more better world outlook.

3

ADVERB————————————————————adv

An adverb modifies (describes) a verb, adjective, or another adverb. The form of an adverb is usually the adjective plus -*ly*.

> WRONG: Sarah proofreads *accurate*.
> RIGHT: Sarah proofreads *accurately*.

The following list details some common problems with adverbs:

1. Do not confuse *good* and *well*. When modifying a verb, do not use *good* if what you mean is *well*. *Well* is an adverb without an -*ly* ending.

   > WRONG: Three of the five applicants did *good* in their interviews.
   > RIGHT: Three of the five applicants did *well* in their interviews.

2. Do not misuse *sure* and *real*. These words are often used informally as adverbs, but even adding -*ly* will not usually clear up the awkwardness they create.

   > AWKWARD: I am *sure* glad you got in touch with me.
   > STILL AWKWARD: I am *surely* glad you got in touch with me.
   > IMPROVED: I am *very* glad you got in touch with me.
   > AWKWARD: The new typewriters function *real* well.
   > STILL AWKWARD: The new typewriters function *really* well.
   > IMPROVED: The new typewriters function *remarkably* (or *quite*, or *exceptionally*, or *unusually*) well.

NOTE: On the use of **conjunctive adverbs** such as *however, indeed, then*, and *therefore*, see **Semicolon.**

● Using Adverbs Appropriately

In the following sentences, circle the errors involving the misuse of adverbs. Write the proper form in the space provided. If a sentence is correct as it stands, write "C" in the blank.

EXAMPLE: ____very____ It was (real) decent of her to forgive us for being late.

_____ 1. Right into this century, managing a household dragged merciless on women's muscles.

___very___ 2. Not real long ago, about half of American women lived exhausting lives on farms.

___awfully___ 3. The typical farmer's wife worked awful hard, a ten-hour day in winter and a thirteen-hour day in summer.

___comparatively___ 4. As late as 1920, interior plumbing on American farms was still comparative rare.

_____ 5. Can anyone say how exhaustedly rural women must have felt when, until recently, they had to carry water to the house each day in addition to all their other chores?

_____ 6. The typically farmer's wife had to fetch water; cook meals; wash laundry; bathe children; make soap, brooms, and clothing; and tend garden, chickens, and cows.

_____ 7. The farm wife felt even more badly than her small-town sister about using the newfangled canned goods to shorten kitchen chores.

_____ 8. The farm woman cooked wonderful but spent long, tedious hours in food preparation.

_____ 9. Farm wives looked forward eagerly to church services or even to a Grange meeting as a diversion from their drudgery.

5

_____ 10. Labor-saving devices sure began to lighten the burdens of middle-class American women in the late nineteenth century, but not enough to compensate for the loss of servant girls increasingly lured to factories and shops.

AGREEMENT————————————————————agr

In any clause or sentence, the verb should agree in number with its subject. If the subject is singular, its verb should be singular. If the subject is plural, its verb should be plural. Also, pronouns should agree with their antecedents. The antecedent is the word for which the pronoun stands.

SUBJECT-VERB AGREEMENT

In the present tense, all verbs end the same in both the singular and the plural—except for the third-person singular, where an -s is added. The third-person singular pronouns are *he, she,* and *it:* "He wakes, she wakes, it wakes." Most of the time you will be using words replaceable by *he, she,* or *it:* "George wakes; *Clare* wakes; *the cat* wakes." But notice that the verb still ends in -*s.*

All other pronouns, singular or plural, agree with the verb without the -*s:* "I *work;* we *work,* you *work.*" Plural words that can be replaced by the pronoun *they* also agree with the verb without the -*s:* The *machines* work.

In simple sentences, you can readily see how all third-person singular subjects take (agree with) -*s* verbs and how all other subjects take the form without -*s:*

He always *strives* for perfection.
Eleanor plays the violin.
They fear their luck has run out.
We demand better working conditions.

Only the subject can govern the verb; other words cannot affect the verb. To find the subject easily, apply the following hints:

1. The object of a preposition cannot be the subject:

   EXAMPLE: This *report* on automobile accidents *is* not up to date. (*Report* is the subject, not *accidents. Accidents* is the object of the preposition *on* in the prepositional phrase *on automobile accidents. Report* takes the singular verb *is.*)

2. *There, here,* and *where* are not subjects. When these words come before the verb, the subject follows the verb:

   EXAMPLE: Where *are* the *snows* of yesterday? (*Snows* is the subject and takes the plural verb *are.*)

3. Subjects and verbs cannot cross comma lines:

   EXAMPLE: The present *report,* as well as the attached support documents, *was* written in record time. (The word *documents* does not make the subject plural. *Documents* has nothing to do with the subject because it is located inside a set of commas, and the verb stands outside that set of commas.)

4. Subjects connected by *and* are plural:

   EXAMPLE: The *Loch Ness Monster* and a *flying saucer have* much in common.

5. When subjects are connected by *or, nor, either . . . or,* or *neither . . . nor,* make the verb agree with the nearest subject:

EXAMPLE: Neither the setting nor the *characters were* very interesting.
EXAMPLE: Neither the characters nor the *setting was* very interesting.

PRONOUN-ANTECEDENT AGREEMENT

The antecedent is the word that a pronoun stands for. A singular antecedent takes a singular pronoun. A plural antecedent takes a plural pronoun.

EXAMPLE: His *memory* seems to have lost *its* former accuracy. (*Memory* is singular and takes the singular pronoun *its.)*
EXAMPLE: My lucky *friends* cashed in *their* winning lottery ticket. (*Friends* is plural and takes the plural pronoun *their.)*

Sexist Pronouns

A special problem in the use of pronouns may occur when the following words are used as antecedents: *each, every, everyone, everybody, everything, someone, somebody, anyone, anybody, no one, nobody, either, neither, another.* Although they may occur in a sentence as antecedents, these words are themselves singular pronouns and should be referred to by singular pronouns.

EXAMPLE: *Each* of us knows *his* job. (The use of *his* assumes that *us* consists entirely of males.)
EXAMPLE: *Each* of the women presented *her* opinion.

NOTE: When any of these antecedents stands for a group of both men and women, you have several options:

1. You may use a double pronoun: "Each of us knows *his or her* job well." Since double references can get cumbersome if overused, try alternate ways to represent both male and female in a group.
2. Leave out the pronouns entirely where possible:

CORRECT: Everyone made *his or her* presentation.
BETTER: Everyone made a presentation.

3. Use plurals where possible:

CORRECT: Everyone made *his or her* presentation.
BETTER: *All managers* made *their* presentations.

● A. Correcting Errors in Subject-Verb Agreement

Underline the simple subject and verb in each sentence or clause. If the verb does not agree with the subject, circle the verb and write the correct form in the space provided. If the sentence or clause is correct as it stands, write "C' in the space.

EXAMPLE: ___die/c___ By one estimate, two of every five deer (dies) because of hunters, many of whom hunt out of season.

___eats/c___ 1. A white-tailed deer, like most large animals, (eat) a great deal, and many times food is in short supply.

___are___ 2. Honeysuckle, clover, soybeans, and an occasional wild crab apple (is) what a deer enjoys most.

___is___ 3. One of the distinguishing characteristics of deer (are) the many colors their coats will change into during a year.

___C___ 4. Few deer anywhere die of old age; either hunters or winter storms get most before they are three years old.

_____ 5. Civilization causes the deer to migrate to unpopulated areas where overfeeding and limited grazing land leads to starvation for many.

___comes___ 6. After the opening of hunting season come the invasion of armies of hunters.

___take___ 7. Over thirteen million hunters, using everything from crossbows to high-powered rifles, takes a heavy toll every autumn.

___is___ 8. Neither an instinctive fear of human beings nor an extraordinary sense of hearing are sufficient defense against hunters.

_____ 9. An effective set of deer-hunting rules and regulations promote a balance between the size of the herd and the animals' food supply.

___keeps___ 10. Hunger for everything from poison ivy to tree bark to field corn keep the deer roving.

9

B. Correcting Errors in Pronoun-Antecedent Agreement

If any pronoun in the following sentences does not agree with its antecedent, circle either the pronoun or its antecedent—whichever you wish to change—and write the correct form above it. Then draw an arrow from pronoun to antecedent. (You may also have to change an occasional verb to make it agree with a changed pronoun or antecedent.)

EXAMPLE: It is hard to believe that a person will deliberately try to sabotage their own success.

people

1. Psychologists who study self-defeating habits see it as a sign of deep emotional trouble.

2. Strangely enough, a person may actually "profit" from ensuring their own failure in school, work, or human relationships.

3. You may find a certain kind of loss or failure acceptable if they enable you to avoid an even more menacing defeat.

4. Missing exams, for instance, may be a student's way to avoid the risk of actually failing it.

5. If someone fails to show up for a job interview, they never have to feel they have been rejected.

6. Even accidents may be preferred if it helps people avoid a fate imagined to be worse.

7. Minor excuse making is normal, but to rely on them excessively is self-imprisoning.

8. A person may sometimes undermine themselves at the moment of a triumph they feel is undeserved.

9. A pathological excuse, unlike normal ones, will often appear too elaborate for the deed they cover.

10. The more you use excuses, the more it traps you.

10

C. Avoiding *"His or Her"* Constructions

In each of the following sentences, you will find the awkward "his or her" construction. Rewrite each sentence, keeping the meaning of the sentence but eliminating the use of *his* or *her.*

EXAMPLE: Each member of our coed volleyball team is required to take his or her turn serving.

REVISION: All members of our coed volleyball team are required to take *their turns* serving.

OR: Each member of our coed volleyball team is required to take a *turn* serving.

1. For hygienic reasons, each member of a family should have his or her own toothbrush.

_____

_____

2. Marriage counselors sometimes recommend that, for newlyweds to avoid money quarrels, they should each have his or her personal bank account.

_____

_____

3. Each of us must choose his or her own path in life.

_____

4. Every moviegoer left the theater with a smile on his or her face.

_____

5. Each person should have his or her own program of daily exercise.

_____

APOSTROPHE———————————ap, apos

The apostrophe ['] is used to show (1) contraction, (2) ownership, and (3) the plural of letters, abbreviations, and numbers.

CONTRACTIONS

Although you should avoid contractions (I'm, can't, don't) in formal writing, you will occasionally want to use them in **informal** settings. Use an apostrophe to stand for the parts of words missing in a contraction: *I'd* (*I would* or *I had*), *we've* (*we have*), *aren't* (*are not*). A common error is to place the apostrophe where two words are joined: *Could'nt* is wrong, whereas *couldn't* is right.

Do not confuse *its* and *it's*. *Its* is a possessive pronoun, and *it's* is a contraction of two words (*it is* or *it has*).

WRONG: *Its* time for a change.
RIGHT: *It's* time for a change. (*It's* means *it is*).

WRONG: The company honored *it's* vice-president.
RIGHT: The company honored *its* vice-president. (*Its* means *belonging to it,* that is, to the company.)

OWNERSHIP

Should you write *attorneys* or *attorney's*? If you mean more than one attorney, a simple plural, write *attorneys*: "The company has fifteen full-time attorneys." But if the idea of ownership is involved, write *attorney's,* which is the possessive case and means "belonging to" or "of" an attorney: "The attorney's office was neater than her car."

Simple Test for the Possessive Case

Put the word that is giving you trouble into an "of" phrase. Should you write *dogs bone* or *dog's bone*? If an "of" phrase—bone of the dog—sounds logical, then use the apostrophe: *dog's bone.* If you are talking about more than one dog, however, use the following two suggestions to distinguish between the possessive singular and the possessive plural:

1. *Possessive Singular:* add -'s. "The *dog's* bone" means "the bone of the dog" (one dog).
2. *Possessive Plural:* add -s'. "The *dogs'* bones" means "the bones of the dogs" (several dogs). (In English, a number of plurals do not end in -s. In the possessive, treat them like the singular: *children's.*)

NOTE: Nouns whose **spelling** changes in the plural are no exception to the rule: *Company's, society's* (possessive singular): "Survival is a society's basic goal" [goal of a society].

Companies', societies' (possessive plural): "Our companies' fears are unfounded" [the fears of our companies].

Avoid misspellings like *companie's, societie's.*

PLURALS OF LETTERS, ABBREVIATIONS, AND NUMBERS

Use the apostrophe for the following items. Once you choose a style, stick to it throughout that piece of writing.

1. *Plurals of Lowercase Letters:* p's and q's. Plurals of capital letters allow you a choice: Qs or Q's. Use *A's, I's,* and *U's* to avoid confusion with the words *As, Is,* and *Us.*
2. *Plurals of Abbreviations That Include Periods:* M.B.A.'s, Ph.D's. Abbreviations with no periods allow you either of two options—VIPs or VIP's.
3. *Plurals of Numbers:* Here, again, you have two options: 20's or 20s, 1980's or 1980s.

● Adding or Removing Apostrophes as Needed

Each of the following sentences contains several errors involving the use or omission of apostrophes. Add apostrophes that are missing, and circle those that should be removed.

EXAMPLE: The two C.P.A.s' offices were located in the city's oldest building.

1. Mrs. Simpsons brother didnt enjoy his two weeks stay in Wakefield refinishing his sisters boat because of this summers unseasonably rainy weather.

2. The guests at the mayors twin daughters birthday party were all made to feel like VIP's'.

3. At the Rotary Clubs annual auction, Dads contribution consisted of two complete sets of Charles Dickens' novels, which were'nt in the best of condition.

4. Both of this hospitals head R.N.s resigned after twenty years service because of irreconcilable disputes' with the administration.

5. Jane's job last summer was designing period costumes of the 1600s' and the 1930s' for the two local theater companie's production's of Arthur Millers *Crucible* and John Steinbecks *Of Mice and Men.*

14

CAPITALIZATION——————————— cap

Use capital letters (the uppercase letters on your typewriter—X, Y, Z—as opposed to the lowercase letters—x, y, z) in the following circumstances:

1. Capitalize all proper names. Proper names are the names of specific persons (*James Dempsey*), nationalities and languages (*Chinese*), places (*California*), certain things (*Bunsen burner*), institutions (*Ramsey High School*), organizations (the *United Nations*), and famous historical events (the *French Revolution*). If you are not sure, consult a recent dictionary made for college use.

2. Capitalize the first letter of the first word of every sentence. This rule includes every quoted sentence:

   He announced, "*The* winner is William Gould."

3. For the titles of books, movies, plays, articles, short stories, poems, and songs, capitalize the following: (1) the first word; and (2) every word except short (one to four letters) prepositions, conjunctions, and articles:

   Sons and Lovers (book), *The Man with Two Brains* (movie), *You Can't Take It with You* (play), "Aquatic Plant Life of Lake Zoar" (article), "Lost in the Funhouse" (story), "Acquainted with the Night" (poem), "Lucy in the Sky with Diamonds" (song).

   NOTE: If you do not know what titles to underline (italicize) and what to quote, see *Italics* and *Quotation Marks*.

   Do **not** capitalize in the following situations:

1. The word *the* at the beginning of institutions and organizations: the Red Cross, the U.S. Coast Guard.
2. Names of seasons: summer, winter, spring, fall.
3. Academic years: junior year, senior year.
4. Academic subjects: "I am studying history." But do capitalize a specific course name: "I am taking American History 101."
5. Family relationships, unless understood as proper names: "I said hello to my uncle Bill." "Hello, Uncle Bill" is also correct.
6. Compass directions: "We are moving back east." But if the direction is the name of a geographical region, do capitalize: "We are moving back to the East."
7. The common names that follow brand names: "A Singer sewing machine," *not* "A Singer Sewing Machine."

● **Eliminating Errors in Capitalization**

The following sentences contain errors in capitalization. Circle the errors and write the correct forms above them.

EXAMPLE: We are going to New York City to see the Chinese new year's Parade.

1. The cold war grew directly out of World war II.
2. When you visit new york, be sure to see the American museum of natural history.
3. Ancient Carthage was destroyed by roman invaders in 146 b.c.
4. She asked me, "how hard did you study for the History exam?"
5. My Aunt Harriet always goes South in the Winter.
6. She stayed up late to watch the hitchcock thriller *North By Northwest.*
7. We are planning to visit the Guggenheim museum on Sunday.
8. In 218 B.C., the carthaginian General hannibal nearly vanquished rome.
9. Almost half the Graduate Mathematics students in the United States are foreign.
10. The Spanish civil war aroused the passions of all of europe.
11. For a time, the beatles followed the maharishi, an indian Guru.
12. On the fourth of July, I drove my Ford Truck up to cape Cod.
13. If you need a History course, I recommend History 302.
14. My old Hoover Vacuum Cleaner has never failed me.
15. The American Microchip Industry is under heavy assault from japanese competitors.
16. Extra-Terrestrials may be unable to grasp newtonian mechanics.
17. Of all the seasons, I like early Fall the best.
18. The Empire State building used to be the tallest building in the world.
19. E.M. Forster's novel *A Passage To India* concerns indian and british relations.
20. A *Yuppie* is a Young Urban Professional.

16

CASE —————————————————— case

Many of the errors you make in **case** are carryovers of informal speech patterns into the more formal situation of writing, where a high degree of grammatical accuracy is usually expected.

Case is the form a pronoun takes when performing a certain role in a sentence. Three cases exist in English: the subjective case, the objective case, and the possessive case. (For nouns in the possessive case, see *Apostrophe*.) How do you know what case to use for a particular pronoun? That depends mainly on your ability to recognize the subjects and objects in sentences. You probably have fewest problems with the possessive case, and those are usually spelling problems.

In a simple sentence like "She hired him," we see the typical English sentence pattern: Subject(*She*) + Verb(*hired*) + Direct Object(*him*). To use case correctly, use the subjective case in positions occupied by subjects, and the objective case in positions occupied by objects. Two other sentence positions occupied by objects are important to note: indirect objects and objects of prepositions. Verbs may have both direct objects and indirect objects: "She gave *him* (*her, me, us, . . .*) a job." You can tell when *him* is an indirect object if you can "translate" it to mean *to him* or *for him*. She gave *him* a job = She gave a job to *him*. Another position for objects is after prepositions (*by, for, of, to, with,* and so on). When the object of a preposition is a pronoun, it must be in the objective case: "They voted for *him* and *me*"; ". . . for *whom* the bell tolls."

Note the following sentences which are analyzed for uses of case:

SENTENCE 1: I wrote her a letter about him asking her several important questions.
ANALYSIS: *I* [Subj.] *wrote* [Vb.] *her* [Ind. Obj.] a *letter* [Dir. Obj.] *about* [Prep.] *him* [Obj. of Prep.] asking *her* [Ind. Obj.] several important *questions* [Dir. Obj.].

SENTENCE 2: I urged her to send me a reply with an extra copy for him.
ANALYSIS: *I* [Subj.] *urged* [Vb.] *her* [Dir. Obj.] *to send* [Vb.] *me* [Ind. Obj.] a *reply* [Dir. Obj.] *with* [Prep.] an extra *copy* [Obj. of Prep.] *for* [Prep.] *him* [Obj. of Prep.].

COMMON CASE PROBLEMS

1. *The Double Subject:*   Do not use the objective case in double subjects:

   WRONG: *Him* and Claire rehearsed the duet.
   RIGHT: *He* and Claire rehearsed the duet. (The subjective case *he* is correct. The test for the correct case is to drop "and Claire." "Him . . . rehearsed" sounds wrong.)

2. *The Double Object:*   Do not use the subjective case in double objects:

   WRONG: Kate telephoned both Suzanne and *he*.
   RIGHT: Kate telephoned both Suzanne and *him*. (*Him* is a direct object. The test for the correct case is to drop "both Suzanne and." "Telephoned . . . he" sounds wrong.)

   WRONG: Bill gave her and *I* the information.
   RIGHT: Bill gave her and *me* the information. (*Me* is an indirect object.)
   WRONG: They returned the album to Myra and *I*.
   RIGHT: They returned the album to Myra and *me*. (*Me* is the object of a preposition.)

3. *Pronoun + Appositive as Subject:*   Use the subjective case for sentences beginning with a pronoun plus an appositive in the subject position:

WRONG: *Us* students are very practical people.
RIGHT: *We* students are very practical people. (*Students,* part of the subject of this sentence, is an **appositive,** a noun that renames or identifies the noun or pronoun before it. If you drop out the appositive *students,* you can see that "Us . . . are very practical" sounds wrong.)

4. *Than/As + Pronoun:*   Use the subjective case for comparisons ending with a pronoun intended as a subject:

WRONG: Hilary skates better than *me.*
RIGHT: Hilary skates better than *I.* (The sentence would logically continue as "Hilary skates better than *I do*" or "than *I skate.*" The subjective case—*I*—is needed because the pronoun after *than* is the subject of an elliptical—unfinished—clause: *I skate.*)

WRONG: Joan is as intelligent as *him.*
RIGHT: Joan is as intelligent as *he.* (Think: "*as he is.*" *He* is the subject of the elliptical clause *he is.*)

NOTE: If the pronoun after *than* or *as* is intended as the **object** of the omitted verb, then it should be in the objective case:

EXAMPLE: John likes him better than *me.* (Think of the sentence with the full elliptical clause included: "John likes him better than *he likes me.*")

5. *To Be + Subjective Case:*   Use the subjective case for any pronoun immediately following the verb *to be* (*am, are, is, was,* and so on):

WRONG: It was *her* who borrowed my new skis.
RIGHT: It was *she* who borrowed my new skis.

6. *Who (Whoever)/Whom (Whomever):*   In choosing between *who* (*whoever*) and *whom* (*whomever*), use *who* (*whoever*) if the pronoun you want is the **subject** of its own clause. Use *whom* (*whomever*) if the pronoun you want is the **object** of its own clause:

EXAMPLE: *Who* gave me the flowers? (Correct. *Who* is the grammatical subject of this question.)
EXAMPLE: *Whom* are you angry with? (Correct. If you turn the sentence around, you get "You are angry with *whom*?" and you can see that *whom* is the object of the preposition *with.*)
EXAMPLE: *Whom* the Gods would destroy they first make mad. (Correct. *Whom* is the object of the verb *destroy* in the clause *whom the Gods would destroy.*)
EXAMPLE: She avoided *whoever* upset her. (Correct. You would expect the object of the verb *avoided* to be *whomever.* It is not. The object of *avoided* is the whole clause *whoever upset her. Whoever* is correct because it acts as the *subject* of its own clause, *whoever upset her.*)

7. *Whose/Who's and Its/It's:*   Do not confuse certain forms of the possessive case with **contractions.** *Whose* and *its* imply possession or ownership:

EXAMPLE: *Whose* down parka is this?
EXAMPLE: Take the parrot out of *its* cage.

Who's and *it's* are contractions and are used informally to replace *who is, it is,* and *it has:*

EXAMPLE: *Who's* (*Who is*) the culprit responsible for this vandalism?
EXAMPLE: *It's* (*It is*) your last chance.
EXAMPLE: *It's* (*It has*) been a long day.

8. *Pronoun + Gerund:*   Use the possessive case for a pronoun that occurs immediately before a gerund (an *-ing* word used as a noun):

EXAMPLE: She did not mind *my* having a second helping. (Correct. Do not write *"me* having.")
EXAMPLE: We look forward to *your* joining us. (Correct. Do not write *"you* joining.")

NOTE: For nouns in the possessive case, see *Apostrophe.*

● **A. Correcting Pronouns**

Cross out any incorrect pronoun in the following sentences. Then, in the space provided, enter the correct case form. If a sentence is correct as it stands, write "C" in the space.

EXAMPLE: _____I_____ Jake doesn't swim as well as ~~me~~.

_____ 1. Sam and I depend on you letting them know.

_____She_____ 2. Her and her friend are equally good chess players.

_____ 3. With you and me on the same side, we have to win.

_____ 4. With a sore throat I can speak French as well as her.

_____ 5. Both Julia and me are needed to finish the job.

_____ 6. The spoils must go to whoever is the victor.

_____ 7. I forgot to who I was supposed to talk.

_____ 8. Whom do you think shall be the next President?

_____ 9. Whoever he tried to blame had a perfect alibi.

_____ 10. Our love should be kept a secret between you and I.

B. Choosing Among *Who, Whom, Whoever,* and *Whomever*

Circle the correct pronoun form in each of the following sentences.

EXAMPLE: [Whomever, (Whoever)] wants to volunteer for the campaign should contact Ms. Rosen.

1. [Who, Whom] was near the dockhouse when it burned down?

2. Lillian Hellman, [who, whom] is the author of *Pentimento,* wrote the screen-plays for many famous films.

3. The choice will be made by [whomever, whoever] is best qualified.

4. [Whoever, Whomever] thought of scheduling final examinations on the weekend should consult students next time.

5. People [who, whom] live by the sea are plagued by rust rotting their cars.

6. Dorian is one of those people [who, whom], I believe, is never satisfied with what he has.

7. Kara did not know [who, whom] she would be playing against at the tennis tournament.

8. Movie stars [who, whom] audiences idolize are not always great actors and actresses.

9. The only actor [who, whom] the critics praised was Sam Waterston.

10. You should tell [whoever, whomever] you think is interested that a baby whale was found beached at Pt. Weymouth early this morning.

● **C. Choosing Between *Who's* and *Whose, It's* and *Its***

Circle the correct pronoun form in each of the following sentences.

EXAMPLE:　[Whose, Who's] problems have I inherited?

1. [Whose, Who's] notebook did you find under the seat?

2. He is a gentleman [whose, who's] word I can trust.

3. [It's, Its] difficult to admit when one is wrong.

4. The experts could tell [whose, who's] signatures had been forged.

5. The grizzly left [it's, its] great tracks in the soft mud.

6. If [it's, its] been signed, its legality becomes indisputable.

7. She's the one [whose, who's] at fault.

8. She's the one [whose, who's] fault it is.

9. An experienced chess player knows when [it's, its] time to concede defeat.

10. The old carthorse knew when [it's, its] time to retire had come.

CHOPPY SENTENCES———————— choppy

Choppy sentences are a series of short sentences similar in structure and monotonous in sound. Usually they are of a simple subject-verb pattern.

> EXAMPLE: I worked all day. I worked very hard. I was bone-tired when it came time to quit.

Even if you string together two or more simple sentences with "ands" or semicolons (;), they are still likely to sound choppy: "I worked all day and worked very hard, and I was bone-tired when it came time to quit." Ways to correct choppiness include the use of *Subordination, Transitions,* and *Variety in Sentence Patterns;* see further exercises under these headings.

> EXAMPLE OF CHOPPY SENTENCES: Rugby is an exciting sport. It originated in Great Britain. It is similar to American football. Rugby has become very popular with American college students within the last few years. Many colleges and universities do not have rugby teams. They have rugby clubs instead. Rugby clubs usually do not receive financial support from their colleges or universities. Other athletic teams receive support.
>
> REVISED FOR SMOOTHNESS: Rugby is an exciting sport that originated in Great Britain and is similar to American football. Although rugby has become very popular with American college students within the last few years, many American colleges and universities still do not have rugby teams. Instead, they have rugby clubs that are different from other athletic teams because they usually do not receive financial support from their colleges or universities. Other athletic teams usually do receive financial support.

Revising Paragraphs to Eliminate Choppiness

To remove choppiness from the following paragraphs, revise and combine sentences to create a smoother rhythm and to bring related ideas into logical connection with each other. Add or drop words as necessary. See the example given in the headnote.

I. The daguerreotype can be considered the predecessor of the modern photograph. It was invented by Louis Jacques Daguerre. He was a Frenchman. The daguerreotype is different from a modern photograph printed on paper. The daguerreotype image is printed on a silver-coated copper plate instead. Producing the copper daguerreotype takes a few basic steps. The silver-coated plate is polished clean. It is held just above a solution of warm iodine. This process forms a silver iodide coating on the plate. The plate is put into a camera obscura. The camera obscura is a darkened box with a pinhole. The plate is exposed. The exposed plate is suspended over heated mercury. The mercury vapor clings to the exposed areas. The remaining silver iodide is removed with a warm cooking salt solution. These few steps result in a positive white matte image on a shiny silver background.

Your revision:

_____

_____

_____

_____

_____

_____

_____

_____

_____

_____

_____

II. Childbearing practices have changed. They have changed tremendously over the last ten years. Attitudes about childbirth have changed. The delivery room atmosphere has changed. Fathers are able now to be present during the delivery. They are sometimes allowed to assist in the delivery. Mothers may choose to have midwives instead of doctors. They may choose to have a baby at home instead of at a hospital. The harsh overhead lamps have disappeared. The delivery rooms are often painted a pastel color instead of sterile white. One technique in particular has affected childbearing practices greatly. It is called natural childbirth. Sometimes natural childbirth is referred to as the Lamaze method. It relies heavily upon controlled breathing exercises. The need for anesthesia is eliminated. Also, suturing is no longer necessary.

Your revision:

_____

_____

_____

_____

_____

_____

_____

_____

_____

_____

_____

COHERENCE———————————— coh

Coherence literally means "holding together." Other words for coherence are *organization, order, arrangement,* and *pattern.* When your phrases, sentences, and ideas hold together, your writing has coherence. In coherent writing, the train of thought is easy to follow. Connections and relationships between ideas are clear. Major ideas stand out from minor points, and ideas of equal importance receive equal emphasis.

LOGICAL ORDER OF IDEAS

Simply throwing down your ideas as they occur to you does not guarantee coherence. The mind very often leaps ahead of the pen, so give your pen time to catch up and arrange your thoughts in a logical sequence. One idea should lead clearly to the next in an orderly, step-by-step pattern with no missing links. There should be a reason that your third sentence follows the second, and not vice versa.

LINKAGE OF IDEAS

A good writer uses various devices to make clear the relationships between ideas. A good writer provides links or transitions that lead the reader from sentence to sentence without confusion. Consider the links—the italicized words—between the following two sentences:

> Skydiving is a fast-growing sport. *In fact,* there is a new sports magazine on the market this month *that devotes the entire issue to skydiving.*

In fact is a transition between the two sentences, a logical bridge telling the reader that factual evidence is at hand to support the first statement. The whole clause *that devotes the entire issue to skydiving* links the two sentences by repeating the main idea of the first sentence, including the key word *skydiving.* Without these two devices, you would have the following **incoherent** piece of writing:

> Skydiving is a fast-growing sport. There is a new sports magazine on the market this month.

There are four main ways to link ideas: (1) transitional words or phrases, (2) repetition of key words or ideas, (3) pronouns, and (4) demonstrative adjectives.

1. *Transitional Words or Phrases:*

    EXAMPLE: More than a dozen condors have bred successfully in captivity. *As a result,* the chance of their extinction seems remote. (*As a result* is a transitional phrase showing the logical connection between the two sentences. Among commonly used transitions are *consequently, first of all, for example, however, on the other hand.* For an extensive list, see **Transitions.**)

2. *Repetition of Key Words or Ideas:*

    EXAMPLE: Most economists agree that inflation is caused primarily by *declining productivity.* It is the *declining levels of productivity* that threaten the economic base of our country, not the national debt

    EXAMPLE: The conventional stereo receiver is not capable of reducing *distortion* before it occurs. *Garbled sound* must be eliminated by manually adjusting the dial. (*Garbled sound* repeats the idea of *distortion.*)

3. *Pronouns:*

    EXAMPLE: Professor Donaldson gave the assignment last week. *He* emphasized that *it* would be due today. (Both *he* and *it* are pronouns that refer to nouns in the previous sentence.)

NOTE: In using pronouns, be sure that they agree in number with their antecedents and that they refer clearly to an antecedent. These points are discussed under **Agreement** and **Pronoun Reference.**

4. *Demonstrative Adjectives:*

    EXAMPLE: The jury reached a decision in less than twenty minutes. *This* verdict would affect the defendant for the next twenty years. (Demonstrative adjectives point back to previous ideas. There are four demonstrative adjectives: *this, that, these, those.*)

● A. Identifying Linking Devices

The following list numbers the four main ways of linking ideas:

1. transitional words or phrases
2. repetition of key words or ideas
3. pronouns
4. demonstrative adjectives

In the following sentences, first *underline* the linking devices. Then, above each linking device, write the *number* that identifies it.

EXAMPLE: Through genetic engineering, scientists can now produce a new life form
in the laboratory; however, their critics often regard these gene-jugglers as potential Dr. Frankensteins.

1. Many critics fear that genetic engineers are "meddling" with nature. They fear that scientists may let loose havoc on the environment.

2. New forms of laboratory-produced animal life may eventually benefit many farmers. On the other hand, some animal-rights groups regard such test-tube creatures as the ultimate insult to the integrity of animals.

3. Scientists are nowhere near the ability to create life from inanimate materials. Instead, they must start with the genetic material of living organisms.

4. So far only the simplest gene modifications are being attempted. Scientists have been experimenting, for example, with implanting a gene for faster growth in a farm animal.

5. One of the goals of the new science is to repair defective genes in people. Even this goal is regarded by some critics, however, as immoral and unnatural.

6. Scientists have made tobacco plants glow by the insertion of firefly genes. Critics of such procedures worry that these experimenters are violating, in some profound way, the idea of species identity.

28

B. Creating Follow-Up Sentences

In the space below each sentence, write another sentence that logically develops the main idea by using the linking device suggested.

EXAMPLE: Various new ideas are being advanced on the war against leukemia.

However, a cure has yet to be found.
_____
(Transitional word or phrase)

EXAMPLE: Donnall Thomas has been voted in to another term as mayor.

This election was a victory for the conservative party.
(Demonstrative)

EXAMPLE: Anorexia nervosa is a psychological disorder involving a compulsion to lose weight.

This psychological disorder occasionally results in death.
(Repeated words)

1. Two thirds of the world's population live constantly on the edge of starvation.

_____

(Transitional word or phrase)

_____

2. Cola drinks dominate the $13-billion-a-year American soft-drink market.

_____

(Repeated words)

_____

3. Grace, poise, and exuberance are the qualities a young dancer needs to enter the world of ballet.

_____

(Demonstrative)

_____

4. The fire that ravaged Devon's house was started by his cat.

_____

(Transitional word or phrase)

_____

5. Computers can create, store, and retrieve documents faster than is humanly possible.

_____

(Repeated words)

_____

6. Growing tulips from seed is a hobby anyone can enjoy.

_____

(Demonstrative)

_____

7. The race for the presidency actually begins years before the election.

_____

(Transitional word or phrase)

_____

8. I must hold firm to my viewpoint on the Animal Rights Amendment for several reasons.

_____

(Transitional word or phrase)

_____

9. The committee finally reached a compromise.

_____

(Repeated words)

_____

10. Some citizens are responsible and well informed.

_____

(Pronoun)

_____

C. Revising for Coherence

The following passages lack coherence because the sentences do not flow clearly and smoothly from one another. Rewrite the passages by using effective linking devices. Underline your linking devices.

EXAMPLE: Some people feel that public schools have the right to ban certain books from their libraries. *Huckleberry Finn* has been banned off and on ever since its publication. *The Catcher in the Rye* is often banned.

REVISION: Some people feel that public schools have the right to ban certain books from their libraries. <u>For example</u>, *Huckleberry Finn* has been banned off and on ever since its publication. <u>Another book</u> often banned is *The Catcher in the Rye.*

1. Backpackers who show no enthusiasm for preserving the land are now in the minority. Many backcountry areas are "camped out." Regulations are being written and enforced.

   _____

   _____

   _____

2. Cancer has long been the scourge of mankind. The treatment of cancer has gradually improved. The majority of people who contract cancer will die within five years.

   _____

   _____

   _____

3. One of the most important ways we as citizens can influence the kind of government we have is to lobby our state legislatures. Most know very little about their legislatures or even who their legislators are. The term "lobbyist" has come to have a negative meaning to many people.

   _____

   _____

   _____

4. Although we may not always be conscious of it, most of us belong to several different organizations and groups. Athletic teams, school-related groups, church-related groups, even professional associations are common. Many organizations become actively involved in public issues.

_____

_____

_____

_____

_____

5. Capital punishment—the death penalty—has been the subject of controversy for over three hundred years. The number of executions has decreased drastically over the years. Between 1967 and 1977, no one was executed in the United States.

_____

_____

_____

_____

COLON ————————————————:/

Use a colon [:] to point ahead to whatever directly follows it. The colon introduces material of three possible kinds: (1) a list of items, (2) an explanation, and (3) a long quotation.

NOTE: Do not place a colon after the words *as* or *such as* or any form of the verb *to be* (*is, are,* etc.). Keep in mind also that a colon can come only after a complete clause.

1. *Colon Before a List of Items:* A colon should introduce a list of items, a series of things or ideas normally expressed in parallel form, whether single words, phrases, subordinate clauses or main clauses.

   CORRECT: There are three main reasons to shop at Three Gals: convenience, service, and savings.
   CORRECT: There are three main reasons to shop at Three Gals: We keep virtually every item in stock, we maintain a large and cheerful sales staff, and we offer discounts that can't be topped.
   INCORRECT: Three main reasons to shop at Three Gals are: convenience, service, and savings.
   INCORRECT: Shop at Three Gals for: convenience, service, and savings.

   NOTE: The incorrect examples just given show common misuses of the colon—after a verb or preposition—that interrupt normal sentence structure. The correct uses show that a colon comes only at the end of a main clause.

2. *Colon Before an Explanation:* If a very short explanation or summary follows a statement, either a **colon** or a **dash** may introduce it.

   CORRECT: A tourist's life in the Bahamas can be described in a single word: relaxing.
   CORRECT: A tourist's life in the Bahamas can be described in a single word—relaxing.

   The longer the explanation or summary, the better it is to use a colon.

   CORRECT: Growing old in America can be an extremely negative experience: social and political "ageism," unofficial and official forms of prejudice, hound the elderly at every turn.

3. *Colon Before a Long Quotation:* Use a colon, not a comma, to introduce a quotation of more than one sentence.

   CORRECT: The governor's opponent stated: "Fewer people in this state had jobs in 1987 than in 1986 or 1985. Nearly twice as many people were unemployed in 1987 as in 1983."

● Inserting or Removing Colons

In the following sentences, insert or remove colons as necessary for correctness. Some sentences may be correct as they stand.

EXAMPLE: The best soft drink is⊘water. (Remove colon.)

EXAMPLE: I look for three traits in friends⊙loyalty, intelligence, and a sense of humor. (Remove comma and insert colon.)

1. Three basic aspects of personality seem to change little throughout life‚: anxiety level, friendliness, and openness to new experiences.

2. You have nothing to fear except‚ fear itself.

3. Here are four of the characteristics that make gold so highly prized‚ portability, divisibility, durability, and stability of value.

4. The acceptance of paper money in society is based on‚ widespread mutual trust.

5. Some people fear that science is headed toward "human husbandry"‚ which is the mass production of human embryos for experimental purposes.

6. Medical researchers say‚ "Even after a moderate number of bouts, boxers may suffer some irreversible brain damage. The degree of damage is linked to the number of fights."

7. There is one basic requirement for good physical health—exercise.

8. Another promoter of good heath is‚a balanced diet.

9. I indulge in only one form of escapist reading‚ science fiction.

10. There are two things I never mix‚drinking and driving.

COMMA ————————————————— C

The comma [,] has five main uses:

    Comma Rule 1. Insert a comma before a coordinating conjunction that connects
        two main clauses. *And, but, for, nor, or, so,* and *yet* are coordinating conjunctions.
    Comma Rule 2. Insert a comma after sentence parts that come before the main
        clause, especially long phrases and subordinate clauses.
    Comma Rule 3. Set off parenthetical (nonrestrictive) sentence parts with commas.
    Comma Rule 4. Insert commas between words, phrases, and clauses in a series.
    Comma Rule 5. Use a comma to separate coordinate adjectives.

COMMA RULE 1

Insert a comma before a coordinating conjunction (*and, but, for, nor, or, so, yet*) that
connects two main clauses.

    EXAMPLE: Quality ice cream can be expensive, but with the right ingredients you can
        make it at home.
    EXAMPLE: Some ice-cream parlors offer as many as forty exotic flavors, yet chocolate
        and vanilla usually sell best.
    EXCEPTION: Ice cream is delicious but it is very fattening. (When main clauses are
        short, they do not need to be separated with a comma.)

COMMA RULE 2

Insert a comma after sentence parts that come before the main clause, especially long
phrases and subordinate clauses.

    EXAMPLE: *Extending from Alabama to Maine,* the Appalachian Mountains are a hiker's
        paradise. (Comma after long introductory phrase.)
    EXAMPLE: *If solitude is what you want,* spend a few days hiking in the Appalachians.
        (Comma after subordinate clause.)
    EXAMPLE: *Near the southern tip of the Appalachians,* the Great Smoky Mountains offer
        eight hundred miles of splendid wilderness. (Comma after long introductory
        phrase.)

NOTE: Some types of *short* introductory elements are also followed by a comma, especially adverbs ending in *-ly* (such as *fortunately, naturally, occasionally*), and transitions (expressions such as *for example, however, in fact, of course, on the other hand:* see
Transitions for a fuller list). Other types of introductory short phrases need *not* be
followed by a comma: *During the summer* I like to hike and fish.

COMMA RULE 3

Set off parenthetical (nonrestrictive) sentence parts with commas. Information not
essential to the meaning of a sentence is parenthetical or nonrestrictive.

    EXAMPLE: Marriage, *an institution as old as history,* is being seriously questioned by
        many couples today.

EXAMPLE: This questioning, *I believe,* is clearly evident in the ever-increasing divorce
rate.

EXAMPLE: Traditional marriage is, *of course,* still highly valued by the majority.

If you read the previous sentences without the italicized words, the essential meaning of each remains intact. Thus, the italicized phrases are parenthetical, and parenthetical elements must be set off with commas.

Information essential to the meaning of a sentence is **restrictive.** In the following examples, the italicized words cannot be dropped without distorting the essential meaning. Thus, they are restrictive elements and are not set off with commas.

EXAMPLE: People *who believe in individual freedom as the highest value* usually argue
against marriage. (If you remove the italicized *restrictive* clause you get "People usually argue against marriage," a distortion of the original point.)

EXAMPLE: Men *who marry* tend to live longer than men *who do not.*

EXAMPLE: Any couple *with a great deal of premarital troubles* will find marriage a particularly difficult venture.

COMMA RULE 4

Insert commas between words, phrases, and clauses in a series.

EXAMPLE: Laws enacted during the Middle Ages in Europe gave animals the same
legal rights as people, but they could also be *arrested, tried, judged,* and *sen-
tenced.* (A series of verbs.)

EXAMPLE: Scientific experimentation has shown *that* animals have high intelligence
levels, *that* they can feel pain and pleasure, and *that* they exhibit a wide range
of emotions. (A series of clauses beginning with *that*).

NOTE: You may omit the last comma if your prose is strictly **informal,** but be con-
sistent in the approach you choose.

COMMA RULE 5

Use a comma to separate coordinate adjectives. In a series of **coordinate** adjectives,
all adjectives stand in equal relation to the noun they modify. To find out whether adjectives are coordinate (and should be separated by a comma), write *and* between them.
If the result sounds acceptable, the adjectives are coordinate.

EXAMPLE: You are about to enter the *maddening, murderous* world of video games.
(Acceptable: the maddening *and* murderous world of video games.)

Sometimes adjectives stand in **unequal** relation to the noun they modify and are not
separated by a comma. In "a little old man," for example, *old* is psychologically part of
the noun *old man* and therefore enjoys a closer relation to *man* than *little.*

EXAMPLE: A *little old* man stood alone on the beach.

EXAMPLE: Even *small home* computers have video-game programs. (Unacceptable:
"small *and home computers.*")

● **A. Inserting Commas Between Main Clauses Connected with a
   Coordinating Conjunction (Comma Rule 1)**

Insert commas where needed in the following sentences. Circle the added commas.
Some sentences may be correct as they stand.

EXAMPLE: No one advertises the utility of cash and checks, but the supposed
advantages of credit cards are heavily touted in all the media.

1. In the 1960s credit cards were status symbols for they were luxuries rather
   than the necessities they have since become.

2. After the 1960s credit cards began to be issued to almost anyone and many
   were even sent through the mail to people who had not requested them.

3. Some people protested receiving unsolicited credit cards but others
   enjoyed amassing them just for fun.

4. Walter Cavanaugh had an income of only $27,000 yet he managed to get
   issued to him 805 cards for a total line of credit of over nine million dollars.

5. An affluent old friend of mine refuses to own credit cards so she often has
   trouble establishing her financial responsibility.

6. I try not to use my credit cards but never seem to stick to my resolution.

7. A Boston bank clerk told her boss that she rarely used her credit cards and
   his reply was that she was failing to support the American economy.

8. Electronic Funds Transfer (EFT) may be the wave of the future for with this
   computerized system no paper transactions are needed.

9. With EFT you pay your creditors electronically for "Money is information."

10. EFT may be the wave of the future but I can't imagine a world without some
    paper money.

B. Composing Sentences Using Comma Rule 1

Use the following subjects to compose your own sentences using a comma and a coordinating conjunction (*and, but, for, nor, or, so, yet*) between main clauses. (Avoid *so* used as a coordinating conjunction in a formal style. See **Subordination** for alternatives.)

EXAMPLE: Jogging and good running shoes

REVISION: Jogging is a healthful activity, and you will benefit from it most if you buy good running shoes.

1. Smoking and health

_____

_____

2. Sports and schoolwork

_____

_____

3. Natural foods and health-food stores

_____

_____

4. Beauty pageants and male chauvinism

_____

_____

5. Loneliness and the elderly

_____

_____

● **C. Inserting Commas After Introductory Sentence Elements (Comma Rule 2)**

Insert commas where needed in the following sentences. Circle the commas you add. Some sentences may be correct as they stand.

EXAMPLE: If you are ordered *not* to think about a white bear⊙ you will find it difficult to think about anything else.

1. By instructing a jury to ignore something a judge may actually be strengthening the jurors' memory of unacceptable testimony.

2. When an unpleasant thought becomes obsessive it can often be suppressed by focusing on a "distractor," a pleasant thought that competes with it.

3. Although we are smart enough to visit the moon, we still know very little about the workings of our own brains.

4. In fact brain science is in its infancy.

5. Once thought to consist of permanent tissue changes called *engrams* memories continue to elude the understanding of researchers.

6. Centuries ago, Descartes declared that the seat of the soul was the pineal gland.

7. Discarding older explanatory models many modern researchers prefer to think of the brain as a kind of supercomputer.

8. Because of recent developments in computer technology many complex natural processes are visualized as matters of "information processing."

9. Of course metaphors are often valuable aids in furthering scientific understanding.

10. On the other hand, metaphors can also hamper the progress of knowledge.

● **D. Using Commas to Set Off Parenthetical Elements (Comma Rule 3)**

Insert commas where needed in the following sentences. Circle the added commas. Some sentences may be correct as they stand.

EXAMPLE: The search for extra-terrestrial intelligence, which is abbreviated as SETI, is more active today than ever before.

1. Inquiring minds throughout the ages from ancient Greece to the present have thought that life might exist on other planets.

2. Many ancient Greek philosophers asserting that the moon, planets, and stars are inhabited were probably expressing a commonly held view.

3. Plutarch in an essay called "The Face that is in the Orb of the Moon" concluded that there must be men in the moon.

4. Plutarch thought that a moon which did not support life would exist to no purpose.

5. Behind his thinking is the belief that an intelligent being created the universe.

6. The earlier philosopher Lucretius who believed in the existence of innumerable worlds felt that life must exist on some celestial bodies as a result of chance alone.

7. These two thinkers whose views are so opposed set up the two main ways of arguing the question for the next two thousand years.

8. The medieval Church which took for granted God's omnipotence condemned those who denied that other inhabited worlds could exist.

9. On other grounds however the Church denied that God had actually created such other inhabited worlds.

10. For lack of direct evidence of course the mystery remains unsolved.

E. Composing Sentences Using Comma Rule 3

Combine the following sentence pairs into a single sentence using either restrictive or nonrestrictive (parenthetical) elements. Punctuate the sentence correctly.

RESTRICTIVE: Some automobiles are becoming more popular. They are imported from Europe and Japan.

REVISION: Automobiles that are imported from Europe and Japan are becoming more popular.

NONRESTRICTIVE: Automaking has strongly influenced the growth of modern industrial societies. It is the world's largest manufacturing industry.

REVISION: Automaking, the world's largest manufacturing industry, has strongly influenced the growth of modern industrial societies.

1. The world oil outlook is affecting the role of the automobile. This outlook is rapidly changing.

_____

_____

2. Each working day more than 100,000 automobiles roll off assembly lines. These automobiles need oil to fuel them.

_____

_____

3. The automobile had its hey-day in an era of low prices. It was an era when oil cost less than two dollars a barrel.

_____

_____

4. Oil is becoming harder to find. It now costs over twenty dollars a barrel.

_____

_____

5. High prices for oil do not mean the end of the automobile. These high prices took everyone by surprise in the 1970s.

_____

_____

● **F. Inserting Commas Between Items in a Series (Comma Rule 4)**

Insert commas where needed in the following sentences. Circle the added commas.

EXAMPLE: Digital computers, unlike textbooks, filmstrips‚ and tape recordings, open up genuine possibilities for *individualized* instruction.

1. Computer-Aided Instruction (CAI) has been said to lack the scorn impatience sarcasm and prejudice that most slow learners perceive in conventional educational methods.

2. Slow learners often see teachers as tyrants classrooms as prisons and textbooks as instruments of torture.

3. A well-programmed computer can substitute for missing teachers keep a student at a task with endless patience and relate to a student without a trace of personal bias.

4. Objections to CAI center on the high cost of the hardware the impersonal rote-memory nature of most of the software and its removal of students from interaction with their peers.

5. Is CAI a bright promise for the future a method of breathing new life into education or a bottomless sinkhole for federal funds?

6. The term *computer-aided instruction* refers to the use of computers to present drills practice exercises and tutorial sequences to students to teach them facts skill and concepts.

7. The three most popular approaches to CAI are the drill and practice method the tutorial method and simulation and games.

8. Through simulation and games we can duplicate hazardous tasks without risking life limb or property.

9. Simulation programs eliminate the need for human subjects dangerous materials and vast stretches of real-world time.

10. Some sophisticated CAI systems guide a student's exposure to textbooks audio lectures film loops T.V. shows and color slides.

G. Using Commas Between Coordinate Adjectives (Comma Rule 5)

Insert commas where needed in the following sentences. Circle the added commas. Some sentences may be correct as they stand.

EXAMPLE: Some educators consider video games to be innovative, efficient learning tools.

1. Video games are loud, expensive gadgets that many people find a nuisance.
2. If used properly, they can be exciting teaching aids.
3. Arcades are often blamed for promoting an unhealthy, negative atmosphere.
4. To see the banning of video games as the fast, simple solution to juvenile delinquency is to overlook many of the productive, useful aspects of these inventions.
5. It Is one thing to want children to play in a healthy social environment; it is quite another to deprive them of an exciting learning experience.
6. Students with no formal instruction in computers will find the flashy, colorful video game the first computer that they learn to control.
7. In the early game called Pac-Man the object was to avoid hungry, devouring monsters while negotiating a confusing, boobytrapped maze.
8. Robotron's closeup views of people often show nothing but scary, expressionless zombies.
9. Robotron's fans love it, however, for the strong, addictive gameplay it offers.
10. Quake is known for its dark, moody atmosphere and Satanic overtones.

Never put a comma after although

43

COMMA SPLICE AND RUN-ON SENTENCE—CS/RO

The comma splice and run-on sentence are errors due to incorrectly joining two separate sentences (or main clauses, which by themselves are independent sentences). The comma splice joins two separate sentences with a comma:

> COMMA SPLICE: The late James Dickey was Poet-in-Residence at the University of South Carolina, he won the National Book Award.
> A POSSIBLE CORRECTION: The late James Dickey was Poet-in-Residence at the University of South Carolina. He won the National Book Award.

The run-on sentence simply leaves out punctuation between two sentences:

> RUN-ON SENTENCE: James Dickey is the author of the novel *Deliverance* it was made into a movie starring Burt Reynolds.
> A POSSIBLE CORRECTION: James Dickey is the author of the novel *Deliverance.* It was made into a movie starring Burt Reynolds.

There are five main ways to correct a comma splice or run-on sentence. For any given case, however, some ways may work better than others. The following example shows a comma splice corrected in five different ways.

> COMMA SPLICE: James Dickey taught poetry and writing to university students, he also found time to give poetry readings all over the country.

1. Separate the two joined sentences with a **period:**

   > CORRECTION 1:   James Dickey taught poetry and writing to university students. He also found time to give poetry readings all over the country.

2. Join the two sentences with a **comma + coordinating conjunction** (*and, but, for, nor, or, so, yet*):

   > CORRECTION 2:   James Dickey taught poetry and writing to university students, yet he also found time to give poetry readings all over the country.

3. Begin one of the main clauses with a **subordinating conjunction** (*although, before, if, since, until*). See a longer list under *Subordination.*

   > CORRECTION 3:   Although James Dickey taught poetry and writing to university students, he also found time to give poetry readings all over the country.

4. Join the sentences with a **semicolon:**

   > CORRECTION 4:   James Dickey taught poetry and writing to university students; he also found time to give poetry readings all over the country.

5. Join the sentences with **semicolon + conjunctive adverb** (*also, consequently, however, still, therefore, thus*). See a longer list under *Semicolon.* Sentences may also be joined with **semicolon + transitional phrase** (*as a result, in fact, on the other hand, that is*). See list under *Transitions.*

CORRECTION 5: James Dickey taught poetry and writing to university students; however, he also found time to give poetry readings all over the country.

NOTE: Occasionally, for special effects, one may join several *short* main clauses with commas: *I came, I saw, I conquered.*

● Identifying and Correcting Comma Splices and Run-On Sentences

The following sentences include comma-splice errors (CS), run-on sentences (RO), and correct sentences (C). In the space provided, write the appropriate capital letter(s); then correct errors using any of the five ways previously shown.

EXAMPLE: __RO___ An armed robbery of a major bank averages a take of $10,000, the but ∧ average amount embezzled through computers is $430,000.

1. Some computer experts cannot resist computer crime, the chances of getting caught are not very high.

2. In November, 1978, computer consultant Mark Rifkin robbed the Security Pacific Bank in Los Angeles of a cool $10.2 million, his crime was detected only by chance.

3. Several years ago a computer security expert investigated 175 cases of crimes involving computers and found that "hardly any were uncovered through normal security precautions and accounting controls."

4. We would like auditors to be better at catching computer criminals, however, auditing procedures are not set up to catch embezzlers.

5. Auditors seldom *find* a loss, they may confirm it after it is already known.

6. In dealing with computerized systems, the auditor loses the traditional "paper trail", invoices, checks, and receipts do not crop up in computer crime.

7. Significant incentives to computer crime unfortunately still exist, for example, the punishment of convicted criminals tends to be mild.

8. The few computer thieves who are caught often escape prosecution. in fact, the institutions they rob prefer to avoid the unfavorable publicity of a public trial.

9. The banking business is squeamish about bad publicity, after all, their business is based on mutual trust.

 10. The prosecution of computer crime is especially difficult; the technical knowledge called for is simply not available to most police departments.

COMPARISON———————————————comp

Incomplete or faulty comparisons lead to illogical, ungrammatical, or ambiguous statements. Be sure to include all words needed to complete a comparison.

ILLOGICAL: The weather in California is milder than New York. (Weather is illogically compared to a state.)
REVISION: The weather in California is milder than *the weather in* New York.
OR: The weather in California is milder than *that in* New York.

INCOMPLETE: The culture of China is as old or older than that of ancient Egypt.
REVISION: The culture of China is as old *as* or older than that of ancient Egypt. (The second *as* is needed for grammatical completeness.)

AMBIGUOUS: I like sports more than you. (Two possible meanings here!)
REVISION: I like sports more than you *do.*
OR: I like sports more than *I like* you.

● Correcting Incomplete Comparisons

Supply any words needed to complete comparisons in the following sentences.

EXAMPLE: Einstein's contribution to physics was greater than *that of* anyone else in this century.

1. To me astronomy is more interesting than any *other* existing science.

2. The depletion of atmospheric ozone is much more dangerous now than *in* the past.

3. Developments in astronomy have had more impact on society than *development* biology.

4. The atmosphere of the Earth is much thicker than *that of* Mars.

5. Infrared emissions from stars are as important, if not more important than *that of* visible light to astronomers.

6. The magnetic field of Jupiter is stronger than *that of* any other planet.

7. I find a book on astronomy much more relaxing than you.

8. British scientists are at least as famous, if not more famous than their American colleagues in contributing to our knowledge about black holes.

9. The experiments of physicists are as important to the understanding of the heavens as astronomers.

10. A trip to the nearest star will be unimaginably more dangerous than our most distant planet.

DANGLING MODIFIER————————dang

A **modifier** is any word or group of words that gives information about, or **modifies,** another word. A modifier **dangles** when it does not clearly modify another word in the sentence—usually the subject of the sentence. A **dangling modifier** may sometimes be accidentally funny, but it is often confusing for the reader.

EXAMPLE: *When painting,* a model is expected to remain perfectly still.
REVISION ONE: When painting, the artist expects a model to remain perfectly still. (In the first sentence, *painting* is made illogically to modify *model.* In the revision, *painting* logically modifies the word *artist,* which was missing in the first version.)
REVISION TWO: When the artist is painting, a model is expected to remain perfectly still. (The dangling modifier is changed into a subordinate clause that shows *who* is painting.)

Eliminating Dangling Modifiers

Rewrite the following sentences, eliminating the dangling modifiers. Some sentences may be correct as they stand.

EXAMPLE: To fly-cast successfully, the stream should not be flowing more than a few miles an hour.

REVISION: For an angler to fly-cast successfully, the stream should not be flowing more than a few miles an hour.

1. Running to catch the bus, my pants became spattered with mud.

    _____ as I _____

    _____

2. To ski well, the snow should be a dry, fine powder.

    In order for a skier _____

    for you to ski well _____

3. Chilled to the bone and nearly frostbitten, the ski lodge with its warm fire looked very inviting.

    when I was _____

    _____

4. If properly treated, a sprained ankle will feel better within minutes.

    correct _____

    _____

5. Barely catching the last bus home, my teeth chattered from the cold.

    _____

    _____

6. To climb up the corporate ladder, a junior executive's desk should look neat at all times.

    _____

    _____

51

7. Attending live rock concerts requires eardrums that can withstand loud volumes.

_____

_____

8. Having attended many concerts, the Rolling Stones are probably the best group of all.

_____

_____

9. If basted, a turkey probably tastes better.

_____

_____

10. Having taken a speed-reading course, the novel was finished in less than an hour.

_____

_____

EMPHASIS ─────────────────── em

The parts of a sentence should be arranged so as to give proper emphasis to what is more important, and less emphasis to what is less important. The position of greatest emphasis in a sentence is the end. Therefore, place your most important point at the end of a sentence. In a long sentence that has several points to make, arrange your material in **climactic order**—the most important point at the end, the second most important point just before the end, point number three before that, and so on.

WEAK EMPHASIS: None of the children was injured although the school bus hit an embankment

REVISION: Although the school bus hit an embankment, none of the children was injured. (The idea needing emphasis is *none of the children was injured*, which is therefore placed at the end of the sentence.)

WEAK EMPHASIS: The 55 m.p.h. speed limit has saved over six thousand lives a year, has helped conserve fuel, and has reduced road wear.

REVISION: The 55 m.p.h. speed limit has reduced road wear, has helped conserve fuel, and has saved over six thousand lives a year. (The three things accomplished by the speed limit are now arranged in order of climax.)

● **A. Rewriting Sentences for Emphasis**

Rewrite the following sentences in order to give their ideas the proper order of emphasis.

EXAMPLE: Cow worship is the number one cause of India's hunger and poverty, according to many experts.

REVISION: According to many experts, cow worship is the number one cause of India's hunger and poverty.

1. Because the cow is the symbol of everything that is alive, Hindus venerate cows.

_____

_____

2. India's cows defecate all over the sidewalks, break into private gardens, browse off market stalls, and wander through the streets.

_____

_____

3. By letting them graze on small fields adjacent to the station house, the police nurse stray cattle that are ill back to health in Madras.

_____

_____

4. Hindu farmers pray for their cows when they get sick, adorn them with garlands and tassels, and regard them as members of the family.

_____

_____

5. In ways, however, that are easily overlooked or demeaned by observers from industrialized societies, cows are important to the Indian ecosystem.

_____

_____

6. The economic functions of the zebu cow include the breeding of the indispensable male traction animals, the provision of dung used for fertilizer and cooking fuel, and the production of a marginal amount of milk.

_____

_____

B. Combining Ideas in Climactic Order

On a separate sheet of paper, combine each of the following groups of sentences into a single sentence, arranging the ideas in climactic order.

EXAMPLE: Deborah had never been to a race track before. She won over $150 today. She did not even like to gamble. She did not know the difference between a quarter horse and a draft horse.

A SOLUTION: Although Deborah had never been to a race track before, did not know the difference between a quarter horse and a draft horse, and did not even like to gamble, she won $150 today.

1. We shall never surrender.

   We shall fight in the streets.

   We shall fight on the beaches.

   We shall fight in the hills.

2. Mt. Aspen has the best runs.

   It is my favorite ski resort.

   It has the best snow conditions.

   It has the most chair lifts.

3. The dictator executed anyone who opposed him.

   He betrayed his closest advisors.

   He stole from the country's treasury.

4. Basketball requires exceptional athletic ability.

   It is a great sport.

   It requires teamwork.

5. The early American patriots risked their homes in the cause of democracy.

   They risked their lives.

   They risked their reputations.

56

FRAGMENTARY SENTENCE————frag

A **fragmentary sentence** is a group of words that begins with a capital letter and ends with a period like a sentence. However, it lacks at least one element essential to a complete sentence. A fragment, when read aloud, makes no sense as a complete statement, and it can often be attached to the previous or following group of words. If it cannot be attached, then it must be rewritten as a complete sentence in itself or rewritten until it can be attached smoothly to the sentence before or after it.

The heart of a sentence is a subject-verb pattern. If a group of words lacks either a subject or verb, or both, it is a fragmentary sentence. The exception is the **subordinate clause** (see example in "Subordinate-Clause Fragment").

COMMON TYPES OF FRAGMENTS

There are three common types of fragments: (1) phrase fragments, (2) appositive fragments, and (3) subordinate-clause fragments. In the following examples, fragments are in italics—*slanted letters like these.*

Phrase Fragments

The main types of phrase fragments that might give you problems are **adjective** phrases, **adverb** phrases, and **noun** phrases. Whereas a **noun**-phrase fragment lacks a **verb** for sentence completeness, adjective-phrase and adverb-phrase fragments lack both noun **and** verb elements of a complete sentence.

WRONG: The troops charged into battle like wild animals. *Caring nothing for their personal safety.* (The fragment is an **adjective** phrase beginning with *caring,* an adjective form of the verb *care,* which modifies the noun *troops.*)

RIGHT: The troops charged into battle like wild animals, caring nothing for their personal safety.

WRONG: She is able to juggle four apples. *While balancing a glass of water on her forehead.* (The fragment is a long **adverb** phrase beginning with the adverb *while.*)

RIGHT: She is able to juggle four apples while balancing a glass of water on her forehead.

WRONG: The mayor works incredibly hard. *Almost as hard as his secretary.* (The adverb *almost* begins an adverb phrase.)

RIGHT: The mayor works incredibly hard—almost as hard as his secretary.

WRONG: *The best place for hamburgers.* It is unquestionably Blimpo's. (The fragment is a **noun** phrase. Advertising language is full of such attention-getting fragments. In formal usage, complete such fragments with a statement containing a verb.)

RIGHT: The best place for hamburgers is unquestionably Blimpo's.

Appositive Fragments

WRONG: He decided to move to Oregon. *A state that boasts many fine facilities for campers and hikers.* (An appositive is a noun—*state,* in this example—often with attached modifiers—*that boasts,* etc.—which explains or amplifies the noun or pronoun just before it—*Oregon.*)

RIGHT: He decided to move to Oregon, a state that boasts many fine facilities for campers and hikers. (A comma usually sets off an appositive from the rest of the sentence.)

Subordinate-Clause Fragments

WRONG: You may wish to buy a personal computer. *After you find out all the different things it can do.* (Although the subordinate clause has a subject and verb—*you find out*—it cannot stand alone as a complete thought. It cannot stand alone because it begins with a subordinating conjunction—*after, although, since, when,* and so on. Reread the subordinate clause in this example by itself. Notice how unfinished it sounds.) See also the section on **Subordination.**

RIGHT: You may wish to buy a personal computer after you find out all the different things it can do.

WRONG: Learning to write is often a frustrating experience. *Because the pain may initially outweigh the pleasure.* (*Because* is a subordinating conjunction that begins a subordinate clause whose subject is *pain* and whose verb is *may outweigh.*)

RIGHT: Learning to write is often a frustrating experience because the pain may initially outweigh the pleasure.

58

A. Identifying and Correcting Fragmentary Sentences

In each of the following groups there is only one complete sentence. All the others are fragmentary sentences. First, *circle* the one complete sentence, *capitalize* it, and *punctuate* it properly. Next, turn each fragment into a complete sentence in the space provided. In creating complete sentences, add your own words, and invent your own situations, humorous or serious, as you wish.

Group 1:

for the audience to clap loudly

_____

the audience clapping loudly

_____

the audience is clapping loudly

_____

if the audience is clapping loudly

_____

that the audience is clapping loudly

_____

Group 2:

for the tennis match to be played fiercely

_____

the fiercely played tennis match

_____

that the tennis match was played fiercely

_____

the tennis match was played fiercely

_____

because the tennis match was played fiercely

_____

Group 3:

the mother's genuine concern

_____

the genuinely concerned mother

_____

if the mother was concerned genuinely

_____

because the mother was genuinely concerned

_____

the mother was genuinely concerned

_____

● **B. Identifying and Correcting Types of Fragmentary Sentences**

First *identify* the kind of fragment in the space beside the fragment. Write a "P" for a phrase fragment, an "A" for an appositive fragment, and "SC" for a subordinate-clause fragment. Write a "C" if the sentence is complete as it stands. Then, in the space below each fragment, *change* each fragment into a complete sentence. In creating complete sentences, add your own words and invent your own situations—humorous or serious, as you wish.

EXAMPLE: ___P___ The eventual exhaustion of the Sun's fuel.

A POSSIBLE COMPLETION: Because the Sun's fuel will eventually be exhausted, we should begin to stockpile our own.

_____ 1. Because there is a difference between science and technology.

    _____

    _____

_____ 2. Verifiable evidence can be found.

    _____

    _____

_____ 3. It is fascinating to read about cosmology. The study of the universe's structure.

    _____

    _____

_____ 4. Cosmogony being the study of the universe's origin.

    _____

    _____

_____ 5. Although the early philosophers knew nothing of the physical laws that govern matter.

    _____

    _____

_____ 6. For example, a tradition from India that pictures the universe as a giant egg.

_____

_____

_____ 7. Traveling at the speed of light.

_____

_____

_____ 8. Galaxies reach as far as we can see.

_____

_____

_____ 9. Quasar. An acronym for _quasi-stellar_ radio source.

_____

_____

_____ 10. The plausible idea that many stars should have planets.

_____

_____

C. Revising to Eliminate Fragmentary Sentences

Using the space provided, revise this passage to eliminate all fragments:

Although surfing is a sport enjoyed in the southern latitudes for the whole year. It was not until the late 1960s that surfers began appearing on the northern beaches in the winter. Their intense devotion carries over from summer to winter. Surfing in weather most people avoid by staying indoors and stoking the fire in the fireplace. Some wear rubber wet suits, which allow surfers an hour in the frigid water. New dry suits, introduced in 1973. These enable the addicted surfer to stay up to three hours in the water. Icy spray and pounding waves provide the backdrop. For the winter surfers' sport. As in most physical sports, there are plenty of dangers. Ice chunks flow beneath the ocean's surface. Temperatures dropping to below zero. And there is always the possibility of the wet suit's being punctured. The threat of frostbite. This is a condition veteran surfers have come to accept as inevitable. This, and icicles forming on the eyebrows. Surfers claim there is something special about sixteen-foot waves and freezing water. There really must be, but I think I'll just take their word for it.

Your revision:

_____

_____

_____

_____

_____

_____

_____

_____

_____

_____

_____

_____

D. Combining Word Groups to Eliminate Fragments

Combine the word groups within each passage to eliminate fragments. Add or omit words, and punctuate as necessary, but include all of the content.

EXAMPLE: Does a person have to be crazy? Is the willingness to jump from a plane craziness? Jumping into eight thousand feet of nothingness.

A POSSIBLE SOLUTION: Does a person have to be crazy to be willing to jump from a plane into eight thousand feet of nothingness?

1. A jumper is nervous. This is the first time for the jumper. Likely to be a little nervous.

_____

_____

2. The cost for the first jump. This includes instruction. One hundred to one hundred twenty-five dollars is about average.

_____

_____

3. Falling at 186 miles per hour. This is an experience. An experience most would prefer to avoid.

_____

_____

4. There are many skydivers. Skydivers think nothing of it. Nothing at all of jumping from an airplane. The airplane at eight thousand feet.

_____

_____

5. Before going up in the plane. A first-time jumper practices. The procedure is practiced over and over.

_____

_____

64

ITALICS——————————————ital

This sentence is printed in italics, which is a slanted style of type. Words that are underlined in a handwritten or typed page will be set in italics by a printer. When you underline—or italicize—anything, you are giving it unusual emphasis. The following situations require italics:

1. The titles of books, movies, long plays (as opposed to those of only one act), works of art, magazines and newspapers, and the names of ships and airplanes:

   Walden (book)
   Star Wars (movie)
   Romeo and Juliet (long play)
   Mona Lisa (work of art)
   the *Chicago Tribune* (newspaper)
   Time (magazine)
   the *Queen Elizabeth II* (ship)

2. Foreign expressions: *e pluribus unum, coup de grace, pianissimo.*

3. Words, letters, and figures referred to as such, and not for their meaning:

   People say my *g*'s look like *6*'s.
   The object of the verb is *whom.*
   People with neurologically caused reading disorders are called *dyslexic.*
   Avoid the slang word *honcho* in formal writing.

4. Words receiving strong emphasis: "Don't you *dare* call me that again!" he said. (Avoid overusing this method for emphasis; a few times per page is enough.)

● **Underlining for Italics**

In the following paragraph, underline everything that should be italicized.

EXAMPLE: The words effect and affect are often confused.

Several summers ago, I sailed to Europe on board the luxury liner *Mozambique*. It was a restful trip that allowed me time to catch up on some reading. In addition to the *New Yorker* and the *Atlantic Monthly*, I found time to read some European publications like the *London Times* and the *Allgemeine Zeitung*, a German newspaper. Luckily I met someone on board who could read French, and she was kind enough to translate parts of *Le Figaro* for me as well. In it were articles about the opera *La Bohème*, Rodin's sculpture *The Thinker*, and analyses of classic French novels like *Old Goriot* and *The Red and the Black*. Other entertainment possibilities included my choice between two full-length movies each evening. Some of the movies were classics such as *King Kong* and *Casablanca*; others were more recent films such as *Titanic* and *Jurassic Park*. My seven-year-old sister kept sending me telegrams, and in each one she spelled *Europe* without the first *E*. An interesting thing about telegrams is that words like *and* and *the* are omitted, and each sentence ends with *stop*. It was an enjoyable cruise, and the *Mozambique* lived up to its *de luxe* reputation.

MISPLACED MODIFIER———mm, mod

A modifier is any word or group of words that gives information about, or modifies, another word. A modifier is **misplaced** when it is too far away from the word it modifies. **Misplaced modifiers** often cause a reader to misunderstand the meaning of a sentence. As a general rule, place all modifiers as close as possible to the words they modify.

EXAMPLE: Have you read about the couple on a honeymoon in the newspaper?
REVISION: Have you read in the newspaper about the couple on a honeymoon? (In the example, the modifier *in the newspaper* appears so far from the verb that the *honeymoon* seems to be taking place in the newspaper.)

EXAMPLE: At the picnic, shishkabob was served to the guests on skewers.
REVISION: At the picnic, shishkabob on skewers was served to the guests. (The example suggests that the guests were skewered.)

SQUINTING MODIFIERS: A special kind of misplaced modifier is the "squinting" modifier. Because of its position in the sentence, it seems to modify either of two words. Rewrite it to make it refer to one word only.

EXAMPLE: Lawyers who work hard rarely are poor.
REVISION: Lawyers who work hard are rarely poor.
OR: Lawyers who rarely work hard are poor.

Eliminating Misplaced Modifiers

Rewrite the following sentences, eliminating the misplaced modifiers. Some sentences may be correct as they stand.

EXAMPLE: The children found a garter snake searching in the field for their lost baseball.

REVISION: Searching in the field for their lost baseball, the children found a garter snake.

1. Does a person who owns two cars named Clarence live at this address?

   Does Clarence, who owns two cars _ _ _ _

2. Margaret went to the dance with the man wearing a low-cut dress.

   Wearing a low-cut dress, Margaret _ _

3. Only Sue saw the movie twice.

   _____

4. Exercising frequently improves a person's health.

   Frequently _____

5. Economists who predict that another Great Depression is coming soon will be eating their words.

   _____

6. I bought the car from the dealer with a convertible top.

   _____

7. I went all around the city studying about horses in libraries.

   _____

8. Students who study often get good grades.

   _____

9. Large corporations frequently support research that they believe will lead to new products.

   _____

10. Teachers who tell jokes rarely bore their students.

   _____

68

MIXED CONSTRUCTION———————mx

A mixed construction is a sentence that combines two or more parts that do not structurally fit together.

> EXAMPLE: By making weekly savings deposits is your best guarantee of having vacation money for the summer.

The first half of the sentence just given does not fit into the structure of the second half. The second half, beginning with the verb *is*, needs a noun construction before it to act as its subject. But the first half—*By making weekly savings deposits*—is an adverbial phrase, not a noun.

> CORRECTION ONE: Making weekly savings deposits is your best guarantee of having vacation money for the summer.

When you omit *By*, the first part of the sentence becomes a gerund phrase (a gerund is a verb form—*making*—that acts as a noun), and a gerund, as with any other noun construction, can act as a subject of the verb (*is*). Another way to correct this kind of error is to change the second half of the sentence to match the first.

> CORRECTION TWO: By making weekly savings deposits, *you can best guarantee* having vacation money for the summer. (Now the second part of the sentence is a main clause—subject, *you;* verb, *can . . . guarantee*—and the adverb phrase *By making . . . deposits* modifies the verb.)

> EXAMPLE: The reason people are often unable to save money is because they fail to look far enough into the future.
> CORRECTION: The reason people are often unable to save money is *that* they fail to look far enough into the future. (*The reason . . . is* must be followed by a noun construction. But *because* begins an adverb clause. The word *that* changes the adverb clause to a noun clause.)

> EXAMPLE: Just because computer prices are dropping is no reason to keep from buying one indefinitely.
> CORRECTION: *The mere fact that* computer prices are dropping is no reason to keep from buying one indefinitely. (In the example, the adverb clause beginning *Just because* is forced to serve as subject of the verb [*is*]. Since a subject must be in noun form, change *Just because* to a noun-centered expression such as *the simple fact that* or *the mere fact that*.)

> EXAMPLE: Tuesday was when I needed those documents.
> CORRECTION: I needed those documents Tuesday. (*Is when/was when* constructions are frowned upon in formal writing. Simply omit *was when* and reverse the two sentence parts that are left.)

Correcting Mixed Constructions

Rewrite each of the following sentences to eliminate mixed constructions.

EXAMPLE: By waiting an hour in between eating and swimming can prevent stomach cramps.

CORRECTION: Waiting an hour in between eating and swimming can prevent stomach cramps. (See headnotes for another type of correction.)

1. The way America got its name is because a map maker mistakenly thought that Amerigo Vespucci had discovered the new continent.

   _____

   _____

2. Through studying languages is a powerful means of enhancing a business career.

   _____

   _____

3. The reason for the name Cairo (Arabic for the planet Mars) is because the planet Mars was in the ascendant when the city was founded.

   _____

   _____

4. By clipping words, like making "fan" from "fanatic," is a never-ending source of English slang.

   _____

   _____

5. Merely because words in different languages look alike—English *confer-ence,* Spanish *conferencia* (lecture)—does not always imply that they mean the same thing.

   _____the fact that words . . ._____

   _____

70

6. A year ago was when I last spoke French.

_____

_____

7. Just because a slang term may be the first to enter your mind does not
mean you should use it in formal writing.

_____

_____

8. As a result of centuries of borrowing from other languages made English
very rich.

_____

_____

9. One reason foreigners have trouble with English is because of the spelling.

_____

_____

10. During struggles for national survival is when the study of foreign languages
suddenly takes on great importance.

_____

_____

PARAGRAPH ——————————————————— ¶

The beginning of each new paragraph [¶] marks a new stage in the development of your entire essay. Just as sentences are the largest sub-units of a paragraph, so paragraphs are the largest sub-units of your essay. In formal writing, a paragraph does not begin and end just anywhere, as if the writer were playing Pin-the-Tail-on-the-Donkey. The main idea, or topic, of an essay needs to be developed in each of its important **aspects,** and a new paragraph signals the shift to a new aspect of the discussion.

If your topic is broad enough and your essay long enough, each of the main aspects may be broken down into two or more sections, or paragraphs. If, for example, you were writing a short essay on the types of teachers you have known, and you end up writing about five specific types, you may decide to write an introductory paragraph briefly mentioning your purpose and the five types you will treat. Then, you will probably devote **one paragraph** to a description (with examples) of **each type.** Your essay, therefore, would be divided into at least six paragraphs.

The main idea of each paragraph is usually found in one sentence called the **topic sentence.** (The theme of the whole essay is usually found in the first paragraph and is called the **thesis statement.**) A paragraph consists of a topic sentence, or main idea, plus a number of sentences that **develop** that main idea in some satisfactory way through a **logical argument,** or a series of **details** or **examples,** or any combination of these methods. The topic sentence is usually the first one in a paragraph, although it sometimes appears at the end, as a summary of details or examples that come before it.

There are three main organizational features to a well-structured paragraph: (1) **unity,** the relevance of all sentences to the topic sentence—avoidance of digressions; (2) **development,** elaboration of the main idea with enough details, examples, arguments, and so on, to give the impression of full or adequate treatment; and (3) **coherence,** the connection between one sentence and the next in a logical pattern. The use of transitions is an essential means of achieving coherence.

Transitions, expressions that show the logical relationships between ideas, can be accomplished in four main ways: (1) through the use of certain standard transitional words or phrases, (2) through repetition of key words or ideas, (3) through pronouns, and (4) through demonstrative adjectives (*this, that, these, those*).

(For more information, see *Coherence* and *Transitions.*)

EXAMPLE: One of the most significant changes in American family lifestyles in recent years has been the increase in the number of working women. Each year more and more are joining the ranks of the employed in search of personal fulfillment and financial independence. In fact, over half of the adult female population is now in (the labor force)(Of particular importance to the family lifestyle) is the fact that half of all children under eighteen

Rep. idea   *Rep. key words*

72

now have working mothers. The Census Bureau reported that forty-five percent
Rep, key word   *Rep. idea*
of all (mothers) of preschool children are presently working. (That figure) is four

times higher than it was just thirty years ago.   *Demon. adj.*
Trans. sentence linking ¶s.
(This increase in the number of working women has caused a redefinition of
Topic sentence
family roles.) One important change is that husbands and children are expected
Rep. key idea
to do more around the house. In many households (children are expected not

only to do) the dishes and clean their rooms, but also to do the family grocery

shopping, cook some of the meals, and help care for the younger children.
Rep. key idea
(And because a working woman contributes to the family's economic welfare,)

husbands are beginning to share in what was once considered "woman's work":

babysitting, cooking, and doing the laundry.

● A. Checking Paragraphs for Unity and Coherence

Each of the following paragraphs contains errors in unity, coherence, or both. In the blanks after each paragraph, write the numbers of those sentences that disrupt the unity or coherence of the paragraph, and briefly explain why they disrupt the paragraph. For a paragraph to have unity and coherence, every sentence must clearly develop the topic sentence and logically follow the previous sentence.

EXAMPLE: (1) In the mid-1970s, the familiar aerosol spray can was branded as a dangerous weapon that could bring ecological doom. (2) Americans were told that their use of aerosol spray cans might be endangering the fragile atmospheric ozone layer. (3) If it were destroyed, scientists warned that the consequences could be enormous in severity and scope. (4) Trained scientists undergo years of college training. (5) Since the ozone layer absorbs harmful ultraviolet waves, its destruction could mean more human cancer, damage to plant life, and even global climatic changes. (6) Not all ultraviolet waves are harmful. (7) To avoid such a disaster, restrictions on the use of fluorocarbons, the dangerous chemical cans, have been established throughout the land.

ANSWER: Sentence (4) is irrelevant to the topic sentence, and sentence (6) does not develop the idea of the importance of the ozone layer.

I. (1) *Saturday Night Fever*—both the movie and the soundtrack album—almost singlehandedly popularized disco music in America. (2) The album itself became the most successful in the history of pop music. (3) For most Americans who had never been out dancing and couldn't quite figure out the disco scene, *Saturday Night Fever* made it all very clear. (4) Some film critics have seen elements of Shakespeare's *Romeo and Juliet* in the movie. (5) The success of disco was enhanced by the fact that John Travolta's role in the film was a continuation of the arrogant but lovable Barbarino he was playing on T.V.'s popular *Welcome Back Kotter.* (6) As Neil Young once said, "Rock and Roll will never die." (7) Although it didn't last long, the disco craze made possible by *Saturday Night Fever* added some beautiful moments to the history of pop music.

_____

_____

II. (1) For centuries Chinese physicians have been relieving pain by inserting fine needles into carefully chosen points on a person's body. (2) This technique, called *acupuncture,* has many advantages. (3) It has brought relief to patients suffering chronic backache, arthritis, migraine headaches, and other ailments for which there are no known cures. (4) Chinese medicine predates Western medicine by over a thousand years. (5) Chinese physicians are actually able to use acupuncture in place of an anesthetic and perform major surgery without drugs. (6) This procedure enables the surgeon to operate as slowly and carefully as he wants without worrying about drug levels or side effects. (7) Perhaps you know someone who has undergone acupuncture. (8) The patient remains awake and alert, blood loss is minimal, and recuperation is unhindered by any negative aftereffects of anesthesia.

_____

_____

III. (1) One of the best opportunities for learning about writing is to listen to professional writers discuss their techniques and marketing experiences. (2) Because they work every day with the problems of writing and publishing, they can give valuable hints on how to avoid common pitfalls. (3) I shall never forget the suggestion Norman Mailer gave when he was a guest speaker at my school last year. (4) The English Department was allotted money from the university's budget to pay for these speakers. (5) Professors and published writers from all over the United States came to our school. (6) Mailer suggested, for example, that the first thing a writer ought to get is an agent, not a publisher, since most publishers nowadays will not read unagented book manuscripts.

_____

_____

B. Constructing Paragraphs

Each of the following exercises starts with a general suggestion on how to develop the paragraph in question (use examples, facts, causes, and so on). Next, there is a topic sentence with which you are to begin the paragraph. Following the sentence is a series of jottings, ideas, and other particulars related to that topic. On a separate sheet of paper, write a paragraph that develops the topic sentence using some or all of the given particulars and any others you wish to add. Arrange your ideas in an order you think will be most logical and most effective.

EXAMPLE: Develop a paragraph by using a series of supporting reasons. *Topic sentence:* There are several good reasons for attending college today.

intellectual maturity; emotional
   maturity
different ideas and values
verbal literacy; mathematical literacy
improve communication skills
make friends; meet interesting,
   intelligent people

reasoning ability
higher salaries
skills more valued
more productive

A POSSIBLE CONSTRUCTION: There are several good reasons for attending college today. First, college offers the opportunity to achieve intellectual and emotional maturity through exposure to different ideas and values. Second, we get to strengthen our verbal and mathematical literacy and our capacity to reason and communicate with care and precision. Third, while attending college, we make stimulating new friends and come into contact with a host of interesting, intelligent people. Finally, study after study has shown that college graduates earn more than those who lack a degree. This fact suggests that college graduates have become skilled in areas that are exceptionally valued by our society.

1. Develop a paragraph by using facts or statistics.

   Topic sentence: Although never inexpensive, the cost of a college education is rising every year.

   tuition
   books
   apartment rent
   food prices

   dormitory costs
   fraternity, sorority dues
   transportation (gas, airfare)

2. Develop a paragraph by using examples.

   Topic sentence: What was considered science fiction in space technology fifty years ago has become a reality today.

several manned lunar landings	weather satellites
landing on Mars	communications satellites
photographs from Venus, Jupiter, Saturn	supersonic transport

3. Develop a paragraph by using a chronological sequence.

   Topic sentence: Going to the dentist is one of my least favorite things to do.

anticipation the night before	sitting in the chair
checking in with the secretary	diagnosis
the waiting room	X-rays
reading old magazines	Novocain shots
other patients leaving the office	treatment
finally, my name is called	paying the bill

4. Develop a paragraph by showing the causes of something.

   Topic sentence: There are several reasons why teenagers "turn on" to drugs today.

desire to be accepted, peer pressure	society is drug-oriented
societal, family, school pressures	easily obtainable
rebellion against society, family	curiosity

5. Develop a paragraph that shows the effects of something.

   Topic sentence: Television may be a great source of entertainment and information, but too much can cause serious problems.

stifles communication among family members	encourages dependency
the drug of the masses; retreat from reality	apathy
	overweight
fantasy world divorced from reality	violence
commercialism; consumer-oriented	decline in literacy
	one-way transaction

6. Develop a paragraph by comparing or showing the similarities between two things.

   Topic sentence: Ideally, an expectant father has much in common with an athletic coach.

concerned about diet, smoking, drinking, drugs	provide moral support
should be a team effort all the way through	teach exercises to prepare
team effort at conception	physical conditioning
	adequate rest
	mental attitude, preparation

PARALLELISM————————paral, //

In any sentence, units of meaning that are equal in weight should be expressed in word groups that are equal in structure. If your purpose, for example, is to mention briefly your reasons for choosing a certain academic major, the skeleton structure of your sentence is likely to resemble this: "I chose . . . because (1), because (2), and because (3)." The numbers (1), (2), and (3) stand for three reasons, about equal in weight, and are therefore cast in three **parallel** word groups, each one beginning with *because*.

LACK OF PARALLELISM: Sheila chose to major in Spanish because of her Venezuelan grandfather, and she hopes to travel through South America, as well as the language helping her in business after college.

REVISED FOR PARALLELISM: Sheila chose to major in Spanish because she has a Venezuelan grandfather, because she hopes to travel through South America, and because the language may help her in business after college. (Sheila's three reasons for majoring in Spanish are now expressed more smoothly in three parallel clauses. Each clause begins with the subordinating conjunction *because* followed by a subject and verb.)

LACK OF PARALLELISM: If you want to take up jogging seriously, smoking is a habit you should get rid of and you should not overeat either.

REVISED FOR PARALLELISM: If you want to take up jogging seriously, *smoking* and *overeating* are habits you should get rid of. (The two habits you should get rid of are now expressed in parallel *-ing* phrases. The structural gains in symmetry and economy make for clearer communication as well.)

● **A. Improving Sentences Through Parallelism**

In the space provided, rewrite the following sentences using parallelism to improve their structure.

EXAMPLE: To write fiction successfully requires talent and you have to be persistent.
REVISION: To write fiction successfully requires talent and persistence.

1. For the aspiring writer, the accumulation of rejection slips is a rite of passage, a test of endurance, and it proves in a concrete way that one is, after all, a writer.

_____

_____

2. The most important lesson of literature is that we are not alone in suffering the agonies of childhood, adolescence, and those of being an adult.

_____

_____

3. If you want to be a good writer, you have to be a good listener and someone who reads a good deal.

_____

_____

4. If you want to write effectively, keep your main point in mind, don't stray too far from it without good reason, and you should develop it in convincing detail.

_____

_____

5. James Dickey was a poet, a novelist, and he wrote literary criticism.

_____

_____

80

B. Creating Sentences Containing Parallelism

Answer each statement in one sentence that uses parallelism effectively.

EXAMPLE: Describe three superstitions common among your friends.

A POSSIBLE ANSWER: My friends avoid walking under ladders, lighting three cigarettes on one match, and making a toast with an empty glass.

1. Describe three characteristics of your best friend.

_____

_____

2. What are two things a dog might do while waiting for its dinner?

_____

_____

3. What are two things a person can do to be sure of an enjoyable vacation?

_____

_____

4. Give three reasons for liking a favorite record album.

_____

_____

5. Describe two ways people like to get into a swimming pool.

_____

_____

PARENTHESES————————paren, ()

Parentheses—( )—are used to set off information that is not essential to the meaning of the sentence.

WRONG: The reasons I quit school were to earn some money (and to gain some experience in the business world). (Parentheses here wrongly enclose **essential** information—one of the *reasons* for quitting school.)

RIGHT: The reasons I quit school (at least my two main reasons) were to earn some money and gain some experience in the business world. (You could drop *at least my two main reasons* with no loss of essential meaning.)

Not only parentheses but commas and dashes also are used to set off parenthetical information. The punctuation you choose, however, determines the level of emphasis you give to the set-off information. Parentheses **de-emphasize** what they enclose. Use them for material that is relatively unimportant or incidental to the main idea.

EXAMPLE: Newer cars (from 1995 on) are less expensive to repair than older ones because parts are easier to find.

When commas set off parenthetical information, they do **not** de-emphasize its importance.

EXAMPLE: The cost for repairing the car, a vintage Porsche, was well worth it.

Dashes indicate an abrupt change in thought and, unlike parentheses or commas, actually **emphasize** parenthetical material.

EXAMPLE: Older cars—my 1989 Porsche, for example—can be very expensive to repair.

Choosing Between Parentheses, Dashes, and Commas

Insert the appropriate punctuation (parentheses, dashes, or commas) in the following sentences. In some cases, more than one type of punctuation may be suitable. Your choice will depend on the degree of emphasis you want to give to parenthetical information in the sentence.

EXAMPLE: George Washington (the father of our country) was reluctant to accept the nomination for a second term as President. (If you wish, you may set off *the father of our country* in parentheses and eliminate the commas.)

1. The chemical it does not, to our knowledge, occur naturally was synthetically produced in our laboratory.

2. Jonathan Swift author of *Gulliver's Travels* is known for his satire on man's absurd and often inhumane behavior.

3. Weather conditions usually associated with the tropics, heat, humidity, and torrential rainfall, exist in some areas of the temperate zone as well.

4. The laser—an acronym for Light Amplification by Stimulated Emission of Radiation—is now used for everything from eye surgery to cutting tunnels through mountains.

5. Be sure to send your mother (don't forget, now!) a card on her birthday.

6. The library is open every day except Sundays and holidays between 8 a.m. and 12 p.m.

7. Arthur Rubinstein 1887–1982 was one of the greatest pianists of the twentieth century.

8. Artist Yves Klein described by some critics as the French visionary died in 1962 at the age of thirty-four.

9. About 800,000 readers well, maybe not exactly readers shelled out $15 million for Jane Fonda's exercise book.

10. Mankind's constant companions war and economic problems are unlikely to be minimized by political promises.

PASSIVE VOICE———————————pass

Sentences written in the **passive voice** are usually less effective than those written in the **active voice.** Whenever you can, choose the active over the passive voice for the following reasons:

ACTIVE VOICE: Botticelli painted *The Birth of Venus.*
PASSIVE VOICE: *The Birth of Venus* was painted by Botticelli.

ACTIVE VOICE: Writing is the first thing I do each day.
PASSIVE VOICE: Writing is the first thing done by me each day. (Notice what happens in the passive voice: The active form of the verb *do* is turned into a form based on the past participle *done,* and the subject of the verb [I] loses emphasis by trailing after the verb and winding up as object of a preposition: *by me.* Notice, also, that the passive voice is more wordy than the active voice.)

NOTE: The passive voice may be preferred, however, if the receiver of the action, or the action itself, is more important than the doer.

EXAMPLE OF EFFECTIVE USE OF PASSIVE VOICE: Today's world championship heavyweight match was fought with consummate skill by both contestants. (The fight, not the fighters, is stressed here.)

Changing from the Passive to the Active Voice

In the space beside each sentence, insert a "P" if the sentence is in the passive voice, and insert an "A" if it is in the active voice. Then, in the space below each sentence, rewrite sentences in the *passive* voice to turn them into sentences in the *active* voice. (See also **Shifts in Point of View,** Exercise B.)

EXAMPLE: ___P___ My subscription to *Sports Illustrated* was renewed by me today.

VOICE REVISION: I renewed my subscription to *Sports Illustrated* today.

_____ 1. The injured football player was examined by the team's physician.

_____

_____

_____ 2. I was offered a summer job as lifeguard by the pool director.

_____

_____

_____ 3. Shakespeare wrote the often-produced comedy *A Winter's Tale.*

_____

_____

_____ 4. The political views of a newspaper are expressed by the editorials.

_____

_____

_____ 5. Because of the heavy flooding in Arkansas, a "state of emergency" was declared by the President.

_____

_____

_____ 6. Today's successful vote to end capital punishment was deplored by a sizable minority.

_____

_____

_____ 7. Following the earthquake, the coastal towns were devastated by a tidal wave.

_____

_____

_____ 8. Thunder frightens most dogs.

_____

_____

_____ 9. The sun was eclipsed by the moon at 12:35 a.m.

_____

_____

_____ 10. In most cases, verbs in the active voice should be used by writers rather than verbs in the passive voice.

_____

_____

86

PRONOUN REFERENCE————————pro

Problems in pronoun reference occur when a pronoun does not refer clearly to a specific noun in its neighborhood. The noun that the pronoun should refer to is called the **antecedent** of the pronoun.

DANGLING PRONOUNS

Dangling pronouns have no antecedent. They are often used to refer to a whole idea that has not been cast in the form of a single **noun**, but rather in the form of a **main clause**—even a whole previous sentence. Watch out for the pronouns **which, this** and **it,** for they are the ones most often found dangling.

UNCLEAR REFERENCE: Sean is extremely congenial, *which* enables him to get along with virtually anyone. (The dangling *which* has no antecedent. It is used ungrammatically to refer to the whole preceding main clause.)

REVISION ONE: Sean is extremely congenial, a *characteristic which* enables him to get along with virtually anyone. (Simply provide a noun before *which* that logically encompasses the whole idea of the main clause before it.)

REVISION TWO: Sean is extremely congenial. *This characteristic* enables him to get along with virtually anyone. (The point is the same for Revision 1, except that you now have two sentences instead of one.)

UNCLEAR REFERENCE: The union leaders alternately promised, threatened, cajoled, and consoled. *This* confused the membership about union policies. (Do not begin a sentence with a simple *this* referring to the whole previous sentence. Use revision techniques that apply to *which.*)

REVISION ONE: The union leaders alternately promised, threatened, cajoled, and consoled, a *strategy that* confused the membership about union policies.

REVISION TWO: The union leaders alternately promised, threatened, cajoled, and consoled. *This strategy* confused the membership about union policies.

UNCLEAR REFERENCE: *It* said in yesterday's newspaper that the sanitation union and management had finally reached a settlement. (Who or what is *it*? Avoid the "It said in the papers" or 'It said on the radio" kind of statement.)

REVISION ONE: *I read* in yesterday's newspaper that the sanitation union and management had finally reached a settlement.

REVISION TWO: *Yesterday's newspaper reported that* the sanitation union and management had finally reached a settlement.

AMBIGUOUS PRONOUNS

Sometimes it is unclear to which of two previous nouns a pronoun refers. This situation opens a statement to double meaning, or ambiguity.

EXAMPLE: John removed the oriental rug from the floor and then washed *it*. (Does *it* refer to the rug or the floor?)

REVISION: Before washing the floor, John removed the oriental rug. (Problems of ambiguity are best solved by completely recasting the entire sentence.)

● Revising to Eliminate Pronoun-Reference Problems

Revise the following sentences to eliminate problems in pronoun reference.

EXAMPLE: If you are abducted by aliens, do not give them your address, This may protect your loved ones from similar harassment.

REVISION: If you are abducted by aliens, do not give them your address. *This tactic* may protect your loved ones from similar harassment.

EXAMPLE: When I saw that the two old men had been spotted by the group of rowdy teenagers, I dashed toward them to warn them away.

REVISION: When I saw that the two old men had been spotted by the group of rowdy teenagers, I dashed toward *the old men* to warn them away.

1. Our continuing interest in UFOs is maintained by new books on these alien visitors and is stoked by our love of the exotic. This is enough to inspire uncritical belief in many people.

   _____

   _____

2. William's extra-terrestrial captor told him that he was not in very good health.

   _____

   _____

3. The alien would never be able to get home, which saddened everyone who watched the film.

   _____

   _____

4. As I saw the monster heading toward my unsuspecting son, I shouted at him as loudly as I could.

   _____

   _____

5. John wondered whether the invading Arcturan had implanted in Peter an intelligence as great as his own.

_____

_____

6. The starving astronauts roasted and devoured the alien creature, which resulted in their being charged with murder.

_____

_____

7. When the great-eyed octopod whipped a tentacle out for my gun, I hurled it spinning away into space.

_____

_____

8. In the early days of science fiction, it was difficult for female writers to get published in the genre. This prompted many women writers to use male pen names.

_____ This problem _____

_____

9. Until recently, sexism reigned supreme in the science-fiction magazine market. An article on it appeared in last week's *Atlantic Monthly.*

_____

_____

10. The bulk of science fiction still neglects character development in favor of plot, which renders the genre suspect in the eyes of serious readers of literature.

_____

_____

QUOTATION MARKS———————quot, "/"

Quotation marks ["/"] are used to set off (1) directly quoted words, (2) words used in an unusual way, and (3) the titles of sub-units of a book or magazine—a chapter, story, poem, and so on.

SETTING OFF DIRECTLY QUOTED WORDS

Do not use quotation marks to set off an *indirect* quotation.

EXAMPLE: The professor announced, "I shall be giving a test this Friday."
EXAMPLE: "I shall be giving a test," said the professor, "this Friday." (When the words identifying the speaker—*said the professor*—break up the quoted sentence, they are set off with commas. Each **part** of the interrupted quotation is then enclosed in quotation marks.)
EXAMPLE: "I shall be giving a test this Friday," said the professor. "Please try to get here early." (In this example, *said the professor* ends with a period because it ends a full sentence. A new sentence begins with "Please.")
EXAMPLE: The professor announced that he will be giving a test this Friday. (This sentence is an example of an **indirect** quotation—a **report** of what someone said. Do not use quotation marks for an indirect quotation.

SETTING OFF WORDS USED IN AN UNUSUAL WAY

EXAMPLE: Arnold may not be the brightest person, but I resent his being called an "airhead." (The quotation marks around "airhead" set it off as an unusual term, a piece of slang to be distinguished from the writer's normal vocabulary.)

SETTING OFF TITLES OF SUB-UNITS OF A BOOK OR MAGAZINE

Sub-units include the title of a story, a poem, an article, a chapter, and so on.

EXAMPLE: Stanislaw Lem's "A Good Shellacking," in his book *Cyberiad,* is one of the funniest short stories I have ever read.

To set off a quotation **within** a quotation, use a pair of single quotation marks ['/'].

EXAMPLE: He said, "Be sure to read Stanislaw Lem's 'A Good Shellacking.' "

USING CLOSING QUOTATION MARKS WITH OTHER PUNCTUATION

Periods and commas belong **inside** closing quotation marks.

EXAMPLE: Alexander Pope called mankind "the glory, jest, and riddle of the world."
EXAMPLE: Pope said, "Whatever is, is right," but I heartily disagree with him.

Colons and semicolons fall **outside** closing quotation marks.

EXAMPLE: They called him "Good Time Charlie": he was never there when you needed a friend.
EXAMPLE: Emerson said, "To be great is to be misunderstood"; he did not say, however, that to be misunderstood is to be great.

Exclamation points and question marks belong **inside** closing quotation marks when they belong to the quotation. They belong **outside** when **not** a part of the quotation.

EXAMPLE: He asked me bluntly, "Do you need any help?" (Question mark is part of quotation.)
EXAMPLE: Did you call this room "quiet"? (Question mark does not belong to quotation.)

● **Supplying Quotation Marks and Related Punctuation**

In the following sentences, supply the missing quotation marks and any other punctuation needed with them.

EXAMPLE: Henry David Thoreau begins his book *Walden* by saying "I should not talk so much about myself if there were anybody else whom I knew so well."

1. "Most men," Thoreau says, "are so occupied with the coarse labors of life that its finer fruits cannot be plucked by them."

2. "Men labor under a mistake," Thoreau says, "They are employed at laying up treasures which moth and rust will corrupt."

3. Thoreau claims The mass of men lead lives of quiet desperation; therefore, he chose to lead a life very different from that of the majority.

4. Because great books are read by so few, Thoreau once asked "What does our culture amount to?"

5. Did Thoreau get his ideas from Emerson, who once said "Cast aside the acquisition of material items"?

6. As part of the documentation for the research assignment on Yeats's poem The Coming of Wisdom with Time Sheila read the article Yeats's View of Aging in the Coming of Wisdom with Time.

7. In a horror novel entitled The Shining, people are said to shine if they have the power of clairvoyance.

8. I Want to Hold Your Hand was the first big hit by the Beatles.

9. Maria's so-called cinch of a physics final was so hard that she barely passed it.

10. Two famous seventeenth-century poems about love are To His Coy Mistress and A Valediction: Forbidding Mourning.

SEMICOLON —————————————— semi

Use a semicolon [;] between (1) main clauses, and (2) phrases that contain internal commas.

SEMICOLON BETWEEN MAIN CLAUSES

When two complete sentences (main clauses) are closely related in both form and content, a semicolon will emphasize their special relationship.

EXAMPLE: Fan support for our basketball team has been great; the morale of every player is at its highest.

Normally, you would *not* use a semicolon if you connect two main clauses with a coordinating conjunction (*and, but, for, nor, or, so, yet*). Instead, you would use a comma before the conjunction.

EXAMPLE: Fan support for our basketball team has been great, *and* the morale of every player is at its highest.

Semicolons should be used before **conjunctive adverbs,** adverbs acting as transitions between two main clauses. Some of the most common conjunctive adverbs are *besides, consequently, furthermore, hence, however, indeed, instead, likewise, moreover, nevertheless, otherwise, then, therefore, thus.*

EXAMPLE: Fan support for our basketball team has been great; *however,* the team has yet to win a home game. (See also *Comma Splice.*)

Semicolons should be used before **transitional phrases** that link two main clauses. Some of the most common transitional phrases are *after all, at any rate, for example, in addition, in fact, in other words, on the contrary, on the other hand.* See *Transitions.*

EXAMPLE: Fan support for our basketball team has been great; *for example,* over ten thousand people attended our last three home games.

SEMICOLON BETWEEN PHRASES WITH INTERNAL COMMAS

Use the semicolon to show the clear divisions between a parallel series of phrases when each phrase itself contains a comma.

EXAMPLE: The starting line-up for tonight's game is Pam Keel, a senior; Janet Johnson, a sophomore; Elizabeth Hernandez, a junior; Josie O'Hare, a senior; and Bobbie Stein, a junior. (If you removed the semicolons, your reader might easily lose the connection between the name and the school standing.)

COMMON MISUSES OF THE SEMICOLON

1. *Incorrect Between Phrase and Clause:* "With a record of six wins and twelve loses; our team will definitely not make it to the playoffs." (Replace the semicolon with a comma—*losses,*)

2. *Incorrect Between Subordinate and Main Clauses:* "Although our team has many loyal fans; our recent losing streak has damaged player morale." (Replace the semicolon with a comma—*fans,*)

3. *Incorrect Between Main Clause and a List:* "You need three things to win; talented players, good coaching, and loyal fans." (Replace the semicolon with a colon—*win:*)

Inserting Missing Semicolons and Identifying Misused Ones

● A. In the following paragraph, insert needed semicolons. *Circle* your answers. Draw *squares* around semicolons that are used incorrectly.

(1) Great artists most often leap ahead of their time, they provide the connecting link between one artistic age and another. (2) They have the intuition and the courage to recognize that times are changing; that new forces are at work. (3) Leonardo da Vinci's famous *Mona Lisa* does not possess all the characteristics of Renaissance painting; but provides an early view of some qualities later called Baroque. (4) Beethoven was trained in the classicism of eighteenth-century music, however, his later works contain many of the traits of romanticism. (5) In the twentieth century, some of the outstanding artists who broke with conventional styles include the painter Picasso, who broke the "rules" of perspective, the composer Schoenberg, who defied traditional ideas of harmony, and the poet Pound, who dared dispense with grammatical logic as a means of structuring his verse.

B. In the following paragraph, insert needed semicolons. *Circle* your answers. Draw *squares* around semicolons that are used incorrectly.

(1) Despite the age-old superstition that comets are omens of disaster, they have not always been presented as heralds of doom. (2) The first faithful rendering of Halley's comet was as the Star of Bethlehem in a painting by an Italian artist, a painting that dates back to 1301. (3) Of the six hundred or so comets known, only a handful are as spectacular as Halley's, most are visible only through telescopes. (4) Of the comet's two most recent appearances, the more dramatic was in 1910, when the earth actually passed through the fifty-million-mile tail. (5) Sad to say, Halley's next visit in 1985 lacked the flair of the previous appearance. It was particularly visible from the earth, however, on the following dates: November 27, 1985; February 9, 1986; and April 11, 1986.

SHIFT IN POINT OF VIEW————shift

Do not shift needlessly or illogically between different pronoun or verb forms. Pronouns should agree in **number** and **person.** Verbs should agree in **tense, mood,** and **voice.**

AVOIDING PRONOUN SHIFTS

Number

You create a shift in pronoun number when you change from a singular to a plural pronoun, or vice versa, while still referring to the same noun.

EXAMPLE: A student ought to be aware of the financial aid available to *him,* and *they* should make every effort to find out about new scholarship funds.
REVISION: Students ought to be aware of the financial aid available to *them,* and *they* should make every effort to find out about new scholarship funds. (See *Agreement.*)

Person

Personal pronouns occur in three persons. First-person pronouns include *I, me, my, we, our;* second-person pronouns include *you, your, yours;* and third-person pronouns include *he, him, she, her, it, one, they, them, their.* If it is not logically necessary, do not shift in pronoun person, whether in the same sentence, from sentence to sentence, or from paragraph to paragraph.

EXAMPLE: If *one* wants to learn how to cook, the first ingredient *you* need is patience.
REVISION ONE: If *one* wants to learn how to cook, the first ingredient *one* needs is patience. (Overuse of *one,* however, can make your writing sound stiffly formal.)
REVISION TWO: If *you* want to learn how to cook, the first ingredient *you* need is patience.

AVOIDING VERB SHIFTS

Tense

Tense is the **time** of a verb's action (past, present, and future). See *Tense.* Unnecessary shifts in tense—within the same sentence, between sentences, or from paragraph to paragraph—work against clear communication.

EXAMPLE: Sheila *fixed* her bicycle chain, but then she *breaks* it again. (Needless shift from past to present.)
REVISION: Sheila *fixed* her bicycle chain, but then she *broke* it again.

Mood

The **indicative,** the **imperative,** and the **subjunctive** are the three verb moods in English. We use the indicative mood to state facts or question them.

EXAMPLE: I *went* home. *Did* you *go* home?

We use the imperative to give commands: "*Go* home!" The subjunctive mood is used somewhat rarely in English and only with regard to unlikely future events, not facts: "If I *were* (not *was*) young again, I would live my life differently." The most usual mood-shift error is to switch from the imperative to the indicative.

EXAMPLE: When you are in New York City, *visit* the Metropolitan Museum of Art and you *should* also *try* to see the World Trade Center. (*Visit* is the imperative; *should try* is the indicative.)

REVISION: When you are in New York City, *visit* the Metropolitan Museum of Art, and also *try* to see the World Trade Center. (Now both *visit* and *try* are in the imperative.)

Voice

Do not change needlessly from the active to the passive voice (see **Passive Voice**).

EXAMPLE: *We developed* an organizational scheme after all the preliminary data *had been received.*

REVISION: *We developed* an organizational scheme after *we received* all the preliminary data. (*We developed* and *we received* are both in the active voice.)

NOTE: The passive voice may be preferred, however, if the receiver of the action, or the action itself, is more important than the doer (see **Passive Voice**).

A. Correcting Pronoun, Tense, and Mood Shifts

In the following sentences, correct any shifts in pronoun person and number, and in verb tense and mood.

EXAMPLE: As a child I would climb to the top of Mt. Tom, from which (you) could see the Shepang River. (A shift in pronoun person.)

EXAMPLE: Kevin watched the late night movie, and then he (decides) to start his research paper, which (will be) due the next day. (Tense shifts.)
decided *was*

1. Because of their hard work and perseverance, the lacrosse team was rewarded with its first undefeated season last spring.

2. One should always be wary of salespeople who try to sell you something without a warranty.

3. The player slides into third base but was called out by the umpire.

4. Before going on a long trip, inspect all door and window locks, leave a light on, and, if possible, you ought to notify a neighbor of your departure.

5. When someone does a favor, they expect to be thanked. *people*

6. We knew from past dealings with raccoons that you can never leave food out overnight when camping in the woods. *we*

7. Angela has asked me to vote for her, but I did not yet see reason to give her my support.

8. If I was a bird, I would fly to Bermuda today.

9. The band played its best performance yet, and the audience rewarded their fine work with prolonged applause. *their*

10. I was disappointed when the park police said that you could not fish in the reservoir.

98

● B. Correcting Shifts in Voice

Rewrite the following sentences to eliminate shifts in voice.

EXAMPLE: We agreed that Mary Ellen would do the cooking and that all the cleaning would be done by me.

REVISION: We agreed that Mary Ellen would do the cooking and that I would do all the cleaning.

1. Some students read their textbook assignments passively, whereas marginal comments are made liberally by others in response to particularly challenging material.

_____

_____

_____

2. In ancient India, a famous yellow pigment was made from the urine of specially fed cows, but you can now manufacture the same color without the need for animal intervention.

_____

_____

_____

3. Although we would like one day to be able to exceed the speed of light, such a feat will most probably never be accomplished by us.

_____

_____

_____

4. We spent three hours cooking dinner, and then it was eaten in fifteen minutes.

_____

_____

_____

5. You should first mow the lawn, and then the fence should be repaired.

_____

_____

SUBORDINATION─────────sub

In sentence structure, subordination is a technique by which you make clear the relative importance of your ideas. The more important parts of your sentences should normally be the main clauses. Matters of secondary importance should usually be cast in the form of subordinate clauses, phrases, and sometimes even single words.

Subordinate clauses are clauses (that is, word groups containing both a subject and a verb) that most often begin with either a subordinating conjunction or a relative pronoun.

When ideas are of roughly equal importance, **coordination** should be used. Coordination is the use of structurally equal sentence elements, such as two or more main clauses in a sentence, when ideas have about equal weight. A common method of connecting main clauses, and showing the logical relationship between them, is the use of coordinating conjunctions (*and, but, for, nor, or, so, yet*). Note, however, that the word *so* used as a coordinating conjunction is frowned upon in formal English.

> EXAMPLE: I disagree with what you say, *but* I defend to the death your right to say it.

Excessive use of coordination results in choppy, stringy sentences (see *Choppy Sentences*) because the writer has failed to distinguish between ideas according to their importance.

> EXAMPLE: Bill punched Jim, *so* a fight started, *and* everyone in the bar got involved in it. (The use of coordination here—*so . . . and*—results in a choppy sentence that fails to stress any main idea. The skillful use of subordination puts these ideas into relative balance.)
> REVISION: *When* Bill punched Jim, a fight started *that* everyone in the bar got involved in. (The main idea is now stated in a main clause—*a fight started*—and the two lesser ideas are cast in subordinate clauses, one beginning with the subordinating conjunction *when,* the other with the relative pronoun *that.*)

Following is a list of common **subordinators** (subordinating conjunctions and relative pronouns) that signal the beginning of a subordinate clause:

1. *Subordinating Conjunctions:* after, although, as, as if, as long as, as soon as, as though, because, before, even though, if, in order that, no matter how, once, provided, since, so that, though, unless, until, when, whenever, where, wherever, while, why.
2. *Relative Pronouns:* that, what, which, who, whoever, whom, whomever, whose.

USING SUBORDINATION PROPERLY

> EXAMPLE: I ate quickly *because* I feared arriving late. (*Because* is a common subordinating conjunction.)
> EXAMPLE: I was afraid *that* I would arrive late. (*That* is a common relative pronoun.)

The following examples show means of improving choppy or stringy sentences through subordination.

AWKWARD: I liked her very much, *so* I asked her to go out with me. (Avoid the coordinating conjunction *so* in formal English.)

IMPROVED: *Because* I liked her very much, I asked her to go out with me.

AWKWARD: We ran thirty laps on the indoor track today. The weather outside was hot. It was humid, too. (Short, choppy sentences.)

IMPROVED: Since it was hot and humid outside, we ran thirty laps on the indoor track today. (Subordination includes use of a subordinate clause—*Since . . . outside*—and reduction of one of the original sentences to two words—*and humid.*)

AWKWARD: I read an interesting book of humorous science-fiction stories this summer. A friend of mine lent it to me. It was *Cyberiad,* by Stanislaw Lem.

IMPROVED: This summer I read Stanislaw Lem's *Cyberiad,* an interesting book of humorous science-fiction stories *that* a friend of mine lent to me. (Effective subordination requires thoughtful rearrangement of sentence elements.)

Sometimes a subordinate clause occurs without an introductory subordinator.

EXAMPLE: Here is an interesting book *a friend of mine recommended highly.* (You can recognize the words in italics as a subordinate clause if you can insert *that* or *which* in front of it: *that a friend of mine recommended highly.*)

● A. Combining Sentences Through Subordination

Combine each pair of sentences into a single sentence by changing one to a subordinate clause, a phrase, or a single word. The section **Variety in Sentence Patterns** demonstrates several options available to you when you wish to practice the technique of subordination.

EXAMPLE: The computer is intimidating to some students. They think it is impossibly difficult to master.

REVISION: The computer is intimidating to some students because they think it is impossibly difficult to master. (The second sentence has been changed to a subordinate clause beginning with *because*.)

EXAMPLE: Gomez put on a last-minute burst of speed. He crossed the finish line only a split second before Szasz.

REVISION: Putting on a last-minute burst of speed, Gomez crossed the finish line only a split second before Szasz. (*Putting . . . speed* is a phrase formed from the first sentence.)

EXAMPLE: The decision was difficult. It was nonetheless absolutely necessary for us to abandon ship.

REVISION: Our difficult decision to abandon ship was nonetheless absolutely necessary.

1. His parachute opened. The sky diver knew he was saved.

_____

2. He took careful aim. He squeezed the trigger slowly.

_____

3. He hesitated about doing it. Finally, he plunked down his money on the long shot.

_____

_____

4. She was elected company president. She was the most talented of all the managers.

_____

_____

5. Martha was extremely bright. She had to drop her French class, which dragged on too slowly to suit her.

_____

_____

6. She had to choose between partying and studying. She was unhappy about having to make that choice.

_____

_____

7. Dora is a computer whiz. Her brother John can play five musical instruments.

_____

_____

8. She took a chance. She arrived at the airport just in time.

_____

9. We were tired and hungry. We got home just before dark.

_____

10. She felt confident. She zipped through the exam in only half an hour.

_____

_____

B. Composing Sentences with Subordinating Conjunctions

Write a *complex* sentence (a main clause and a subordinate clause) appropriate for the situation described in each of the following cases.

EXAMPLE: The basketball court at your school is being renovated. Consequently, basketball practice will be held at the YWCA. Your coach has asked you to post a note for the other team members. Write a one-sentence message that begins with the subordinating conjunction *because.*

POSSIBLE ANSWER: Because the basketball court is being renovated, practice will be held at the YWCA.

1. You have been shopping at J & K Supermarket for the past five years and have always found its produce and service to be excellent. However, on your last trip to the market you bought a loaf of "fresh" bread which was stale. You want to express your disappointment and dissatisfaction to the management by slipping a brief note into the suggestion box—a one-sentence note beginning with the subordinating conjunction *although.*

_____

_____

_____

2. You missed practice for the varsity swim team. For the record, your coach wants you to write your excuse on the back of your file card. Write just one explanatory sentence beginning with *since.*

_____

_____

_____

3. Someone has been parking in your reserved parking space at work for the past two days. It is your company's policy to tow cars that are improperly parked. Leave a one-sentence note on the car that begins with *unless.*

_____

_____

_____

4. You happen to be in the Spanish Department office at your college when Dr. Hernandez phones to say she is ill and will not hold classes today. The secretary asks you to leave a note on the professor's blackboard for her students. Write a one-sentence note beginning with *because*.

_____

_____

_____

5. You are a lighting technician for a community theater play. On the night of the performance, you must make some lighting changes, and you need to slip a last-minute note to one of the actors explaining that he is not to enter the stage until the spotlight is center-stage. Write a one-sentence note beginning with *after*.

_____

_____

_____

TENSE ———————————————————————————————— T

Most problems in the use of verb **tenses** involve improper **sequence** of tenses or incorrect tense **forms.**

The tense of a verb is the form that expresses a time-frame—past, present, or future—in which an event occurs. Within each time-frame there are variations in verb form that express more subtle time relations. For example, past tenses of the verb *to study* include *I studied* (simple past), *I have studied* (present perfect), *I had studied* (past perfect), and **progressive** tenses that include the participle *studying* (*I have been studying*). Present tense forms include *I study, I am studying.* Future tenses include *I shall (will) study, I shall (will) have studied, I shall be studying.* And then there are the **conditional** tenses that express present, past, and future **possibilities** only: *I would study, I would have studied.* There are many more variations than these, and as a native speaker you should be familiar with them all, but the previous examples should serve for illustration.

SEQUENCE OF TENSES

All verbs in a sentence—and from one sentence to the next—should be in proper time relation to each other, or proper **sequence.** If the actions in the main and subordinate clauses of a sentence occur at the same time, both verbs should be in the same tense.

EXAMPLE: When I *finished* running, I *cooled* down with a cold drink.
EXAMPLE: After I *study* I *watch* one hour of T.V.

If the action in the main clause is **later** than the action in the subordinate clause, use the appropriate past tense in the subordinate clause.

EXAMPLE: I *understand* that you *have* just *graduated* from college. (The verb in the subordinate clause, *have graduated,* is in the present perfect tense and expresses a time just before the present tense of the main verb.)
EXAMPLE: I *understood* that he *had published* under various pen names. (In this example, the past perfect tense, *had published,* in the subordinate clause, denotes a time before the simple past tense, *understood,* of the main clause.)

Unchanging conditions and permanent facts take the present tense, no matter what other tense is used in the sentence.

EXAMPLE: I *learned* that the sun's ultraviolet rays *damage* skin cells.
EXAMPLE: Yesterday I *discovered* that she *publishes* under various pen names.

No matter what the tense of the main verb, use the **present** infinitive if its action is in the same time-frame as the main verb. Use the **past** infinitive if its action occurs before the main verb.

EXAMPLE: I would like *to see* the new play.
EXAMPLE: I would have liked *to see* the new play. (Although *to see* is the **present** infinitive, it is understood to be in the same time-frame, the past tense, of the main verb *would have liked.*)

EXAMPLE: I would like *to have seen* the new play. (The past infinitive, *to have seen,* refers to a time prior to the present tense, *would like,* of the main verb. Avoid doubling the past tense with the past infinitive: "I would have liked to have seen the new play." Either *I would have liked to see* or *I would like to have seen* will do, but not both.)

IRREGULAR VERBS

Not all English verbs use the regular ending *-ed* to form the past tense (*turned*) and past participle (*have turned*). A large group of **irregular** verbs exist that are among the most common verbs used in the language. They form their past tenses and past participles in nonstandard ways that cannot be predicted from the present tense. *I drive,* for example, does not help you predict *I drove* or *I had driven.* If you are unsure of the correct verb form, look up the present-tense form of the verb in the dictionary, where you will find the other forms as well. A list such as the following by no means exhausts the great number of irregular verbs we commonly use.

PRESENT	PAST	PAST PARTICIPLE
I *blow*	I *blew*	I have *blown*
I *break*	I *broke*	I have *broken*
I *bring*	I *brought*	I have *brought*
I *burst*	I *burst*	I have *burst*
I *buy*	I *bought*	I have *bought*
I *do*	I *did*	I have *done*
I *drink*	I *drank*	I have *drunk*
I *drive*	I *drove*	I have *driven*
I *eat*	I *ate*	I have *eaten*
I *fall*	I *fell*	I have *fallen*
I *find*	I *found*	I have *found*
I *fight*	I *fought*	I have *fought*
I *forbid*	I *forbade*	I have *forbidden*
I *hold*	I *held*	I have *held*
I *go*	I *went*	I have *gone*
I *keep*	I *kept*	I have *kept*
I *lay* (a rug down)	I *laid* (a rug down)	I have *laid* (a rug down)
I *lie* (down to sleep)	I *lay* (down to sleep)	I have *lain* (down to sleep)
I *leave*	I *left*	I have *left*
I *make*	I *made*	I have *made*
I *ring*	I *rang*	I have *rung*
I *rise*	I *rose*	I have *risen*
I *run*	I *ran*	I have *run*
I *see*	I *saw*	I have *seen*
I *seek*	I *sought*	I have *sought*
I *steal*	I *stole*	I have *stolen*
I *slide*	I *slid*	I have *slid*
I *strive*	I *strove*	I have *striven*
I *swim*	I *swam*	I have *swum*
I *swing*	I *swung*	I have *swung*
I *take*	I *took*	I have *taken*
I *write*	I *wrote*	I have *written*

A. Using Tenses in Correct Sequence

For each example, circle the verb whose tense is out of sequence with the tense of the verb in italics. Write the correct tense form in the space provided. If both of the verbs are correct, write a "C".

EXAMPLE: __growled__ As the mailman *strolled* up the pathway, the mongrel (growls) at him.

_____ 1. Because George slams the baseball out of the park, we *won* the game.

_____ 2. When I finally see the dentist, the ache *had stopped.*

_____ 3. Even our harshest critics *thought* that the performance is good.

_____ 4. Although students protest, the university *scheduled* weekend classes to make up for the mid-week holiday.

_____ 5. We had an hour to warm up before the swim match, which *will start* at two o'clock sharp.

_____ 6. I *had* just *fallen* asleep when the telephone rings.

_____ 7. I would have liked *to have fought* in the last war.

_____ 8. We could have sold the car when it *is* in better condition.

_____ 9. After he dumps the fastfood tray into the garbage can, he *realized* his keys were on the tray.

_____ 10. We *anticipate* winning the basketball game because the other team had had a losing streak.

108

B. Using Irregular Verb Forms

For each sentence, put the given verb (in parentheses) into the correct tense form. If in doubt, consult the irregular verb list in the headnotes or a good college dictionary.

EXAMPLE: (to fall) The accident victim had ___fallen___ from a moving car.

1. (to steal) Robin Hood _____ from the rich to give to the poor.

2. (to lead) Yesterday John _____ us on a wild goose chase.

3. (to lay) When he told me what his ridiculous intentions were, I simply _____ down the law.

4. (to seek) We have _____ the truth but have been fed only lies.

5. (to sink) The great tanker was _____ by one little torpedo.

6. (to lie) I _____ down to sleep in the morning and woke up after dark.

7. (to go) The little town I grew up in has completely _____ to seed.

8. (to run) Jim has _____ three times in the Boston Marathon.

9. (to swim) He had _____ for five hours before they rescued him.

10. (to blow) Our agent in Crete was killed because his cover was _____.

TRANSITIONS————————————trans

Transitions are a special group of words and phrases that show how a piece of writing progresses logically from one idea to the next. Transitions connect parts of sentences, one sentence to another, and one paragraph to another. They express such logical relations between ideas as addition (*also, besides, furthermore*), contrast (*but, however, on the contrary*), result (*consequently, therefore*), and space or time (*afterward, beyond, in the distance, now*). The following passage, for example, uses transitions of time (in italics).

> *In its earliest stages,* war consisted solely of battle for hunting grounds. *Next* came struggles for pasture; *then* for tilled or tillable land.

There are many ways of showing the logical linkage between ideas; however, only the more commonly used transitions are given in the following list:

1. *Transitional Words:*   accordingly, actually, afterward, again, also, and, before, beforehand, besides, but, consequently, eventually, finally, first, further, furthermore, gradually, hence, here, however, indeed, last, later, likewise, meanwhile, moreover, nevertheless, next, nonetheless, nor, notwithstanding, now, otherwise, second, similarly, soon, still, then, therefore, thereupon, thus, too.

2. *Transitional Phrases:*   after all, all in all, all things considered, and yet, as a result, at length, at the same time, by the same token, even so, for example, for instance, for the most part, for this purpose, generally speaking, in addition, in any event, in brief, in contrast, in fact, in like manner, in other words, in short, in spite of (that), in sum, in the first place, in the meantime, in the past, on the contrary, on the other hand, on the whole, to be sure, to sum up, to this end.

● Supplying Logical Transitions

Write a logical transition in each of the following blanks. More than one appropriate answer may be possible for each. Remember that most transitions, including all that begin a sentence, should be set off by commas.

Vincent Van Gogh

Vincent Van Gogh is generally held to have been the greatest Dutch painter after Rembrandt. (1)_____ of the more than 1500 paintings and drawings that constitute his life's work, he sold only one in his lifetime. Working for a while as a Christian missionary in an impoverished coalmining region of Belgium, he dealt with misery and poverty daily. (2)_____ he developed a deep compassion for his fellow human beings. (3)_____ he reached the point where he felt it was his Christian duty to give all of his worldly possessions to the poor. The Church (4)_____ thought he had interpreted Christian teaching too literally and dismissed him.

His artistic career was extremely short, lasting only the ten years from 1880 to 1890. (5)_____ he worked hard and quickly perfected his unique style of painting. Van Gogh's paintings are vibrantly expressive—through the use of distorted shapes and violent colors—of his own turbulent feelings. (6)_____ some of his critics regard his work as *expressionistic*. (7)_____ many see his art as *impressionistic* because it captures the essential qualities of a subject—without, however, undue reliance on the objective representation of reality. As to the impressionistic label, he was (8)_____ influenced by great impressionists such as Pissarro, Seurat, and Gauguin. The final two years of his life were lived in states of depression, loneliness, and despair. He felt despair (9)_____ at the fact that none of his art was considered good enough ever to interest buyers. (10)_____ he committed suicide at the age of thirty-seven.

TRITENESS ——————————————trite

Trite means overused, unoriginal, ordinary, or dull. Trite writing results from skimpy thinking or lazy, colorless phrasing. You can often weed out weak ideas if you think hard about your topic before you begin to write. In the same way, you can get rid of colorless phrasing if you deliberately try to use the following simple techniques in choosing your words.

1. *Interesting, Picturesque Verbs.* Why use an uninspired verb, as in "The rabbit *ran* out of reach of the cat," when you can write, "The rabbit *zigzagged* out of reach of the cat"?

2. *Accurate, Striking Adjectives.* Wherever possible, use fewer adjectives, but make each one count. A *hot, humid* day is a *sultry* day. An *old, bent* apple tree may be condensed into a *gnarled* apple tree. Sometimes more adjectives are better—if they enable the reader to see more precisely what you have in mind. A *beautiful* sunset is vague; not so a sunset *streaked with violet and pearl.* Often just substituting a vivid word for a dull word is enough. Instead of writing, "The clown's *oversized* hat made the children laugh," you might write, "The clown's *floppy* hat. . . ."

3. *Interesting Comparisons.* A good comparison often works better than a whole sentence of description or explanation. Comparisons using *like* or *as* are called similes: "The sun felt *as hot as molten lava.*" Comparisons without *like* or *as* are called metaphors: "He stared down at me over *the craggy promontory* of his nose."

CLICHÉS

Clichés are comparisons, metaphors, and other figures of speech that have become so popular, so overused, that they are lazy substitutes for the unique, personal perceptions that good writing strives to communicate. There are numerous clichés. Here is a sampling (in italics).

The Republican victory showed that *the tide was turning.*
I stood there *as quiet as a mouse.*
He was *born with a silver spoon in his mouth.*
The exam was about to begin; it was my *moment of truth.*
That joke is *as old as the hills.*
He was *as phony as a three-dollar bill.*
Their house always looks *as neat as a pin.*

A. Using Vivid Verbs and Adjectives

Underline the trite verb or adjective in each of the following sentences, and replace it with a more vivid, interesting one. To replace a trite *adjective,* you may sometimes need more than one word. Write your substitute(s) in the blank at the left of each sentence.

EXAMPLE: ___*hobbled*___ In spite of his hip injury, he bravely <u>walked</u> up the stairs.

_____ 1. The snake came across the lawn.

_____ 2. The hurricane took the roof off the house.

_____ 3. Martina Navratilova finally defeated Chris Evert Lloyd in the finals of the US Tennis Open.

_____ 4. The Dow Jones Industrial Average fell again yesterday.

_____ 5. The Formula Four race car ran into the embankment.

_____ 6. Our neighbors sent us a lovely Christmas card.

_____ 7. Carol Burnett is a good actress.

_____ 8. The weather was awful all week.

_____ 9. After sliding into home plate, he got up looking dirty.

_____ 10. Woody Allen is an extremely funny comedian.

B. Eliminating Clichés

Underline the clichés in the following sentences. Then rewrite each sentence using vivid, original expressions in place of the clichés.

EXAMPLE: Jerry *took to his heels* when he saw the bear coming up the path.

REVISION: Jerry set a world record for the hundred-yard dash when he saw the bear coming up the path.

1. One way to succeed in the business world is to keep a low profile.

_____

_____

2. To mix drinking and driving is like playing with fire.

_____

_____

3. Molly danced across the floor as light as a feather.

_____

_____

4. Professor Morris must have gotten up on the wrong side of the bed this morning.

_____

_____

5. John's newborn son was the apple of his eye.

_____

_____

VAGUENESS ————————————————vague

Vague writing is **unclear** writing. It is unclear because the ideas have not been thought out and presented in a specific enough, direct enough way. Vague writing produces a fuzzy, foggy impression on the reader. It largely avoids concrete detail and dwells instead in the cloudy realms of generalization. When students write about emotionally charged matters, their writing often tends toward vagueness. They want to express their feelings, but they do not remember that to **communicate** feelings they must communicate the precise factual circumstances that caused them to have those feelings in the first place. Consider the following example:

EXAMPLE: My math professor is absolutely unbearable. He makes learning in his class impossible. Most students who take him are permanently turned off by mathematics, and I believe that the administration should do all it can to fire him.

Although the student reveals these negative feelings, we are unable to sympathize fully enough because we do not know what actual circumstances produced those feelings. The following revision fills us in on the facts behind the feelings:

REVISION: My math professor is an unbearable tyrant in class. He does not encourage class participation, especially discourages questions, and lectures almost incessantly while avoiding direct eye contact with his students. When students do manage to get in a question or comment, he responds in a sarcastic way guaranteed to turn them away from the pursuit of mathematical knowledge permanently. I believe that the man should be fired.

A special variety of vagueness results from the misuse of abstract expressions such as *love, hate, idealism, democracy, progress, corruption,* and *individualism.* Expressions like these mean different things to different people. Unfortunately, they sometimes have very little specific meaning to the writer who uses them—and they may be used out of laziness, or prejudice, as a substitute for dealing with the real issues these terms **appear** to describe. If you claim, for example, that this country is founded on a belief in *individualism,* are you really aware of the concrete facts of American life that bear out this abstract generality—and perhaps of other facts that contradict it? Are you intending to refer to the idea that the government exists to serve the individual? Are you really thinking of free enterprise, the right to change jobs, the right to bear arms? Are you thinking of all these ideas at once, or none of them? To be sure that you and your reader are on the same wavelength, always **define** your abstractions, limit them, and qualify them either in the same sentence or in sentences that follow.

Clarifying Vague or Abstract Statements

Each of the following sentences contains a vague or abstract expression, which is underlined. In the space provided, clarify the expression in either of two ways: (a) Rewrite the sentence, or (b) add a sentence that clarifies the first.

EXAMPLE: Wiggins believes in sound principles of management.

(a) Wiggins believes in financially conservative management practices.

(b) He tries to maximize feedback on every organizational level.

1. You were fired because you were not a team player.

_____

_____

2. Reverend Beard had always been a pillar of the community.

_____

_____

3. The nation's space-shuttle program has made great progress since its recent tragic setback.

_____

_____

4. Professor Filbert is the most boring lecturer I know.

_____

_____

5. I support General Ramos because he believes in democracy.

_____

_____

6. My parents don't want me to have friends who are not normal.

_____

_____

7. Ellen works for a <u>fantastic</u> boss.

_____

_____

8. India is more <u>advanced</u> than China.

_____

_____

9. I gave the dog back because it was <u>impossible to handle</u>.

_____

_____

10. For many years, Argentina has been <u>politically unstable</u>.

_____

_____

VARIETY IN SENTENCE PATTERNS—var

Develop a livelier style by varying the **structures** and **lengths** of your sentences. Good writers are always juggling a limited number of basic sentence patterns, balancing one against another to avoid monotony and to create a pleasing, rhythmic flow. You will find these basic structures easy to remember **because you know them already;** you already possess a bag of tricks that you are probably not aware you have.

STRUCTURAL VARIETY

Virtually the same **ideas** can be expressed through a variety of **forms.** Note how a variety of revision patterns can be used to clarify the basic relationship between a pair of simple sentences:

Simple, Compound, and Complex Sentences

EXAMPLE: We lost the first game. We vowed to even the score the next day out. (Here we have two **simple sentences.** A simple sentence contains only one subject-verb nucleus—*We lost* and *we vowed.* The sentences stand uninterestingly next to each other. Notice how in the following examples the use of certain standard word structures creates meaningful relationships between these now separate ideas.)

IMPROVEMENT BY USE OF COORDINATION: We lost the first game, *but* we vowed to even the score the next day out. (We now have a **compound sentence,** which is at least two simple sentences connected by a coordinating conjunction—*and, but, for, nor, or, so,* or *yet.* Their connection by *but* ties these two separate thoughts into a relationship of contrast.)

IMPROVEMENT BY USE OF A SUBORDINATE CLAUSE: *After we lost the first game,* we vowed to even the score the next day out. (A subordinate clause consists of a subordinating conjunction—*after, although, because, since, when*—followed by, at the least, a subject and its verb—*we lost.* Try substituting *although* for *after.*)

VARIETY THROUGH USE OF A RELATIVE CLAUSE: After we lost the first game, we vowed *that we would even the score the next day out.* (A relative clause is a type of subordinate clause beginning normally with a relative pronoun such as *that, what, which, who,* or *whom.*)

NOTE: The combination of a main clause [simple sentence] with a subordinate clause results in a **complex sentence.** One of the ways to gain variety in sentence patterns is to create a pleasing alternation of **simple, compound,** and **complex** sentences.)

The following paragraph, from an essay by Robert Jay Lifton in *The Final Epidemic* (original punctuation slightly modified), illustrates the skillful alternation of simple, compound, and complex sentences:

Although the idea of apocalypse has been with us throughout the ages, it has been within a religious context—the idea that God will punish and even eliminate man for his sins. [Complex] Now it is our own technology, and we are doing it ourselves. [Compound] Nor is it only the nuclear threat. [Simple] There are chemical warfare and germ warfare; destruction of the environment, the air we breathe,

118

or the ozone layer; and depletion of the world's resources, whether of energy or food. [Simple]

Different Types of Phrases

EXAMPLE: We lost the first game. We vowed to even the score the next day out.

IMPROVEMENT BY USE OF A PARTICIPIAL PHRASE: *Having lost the first game*, we vowed to even the score the next day out. (A participial phrase is a group of words beginning with a participle, the *-ing* form of a verb—*having*. It acts as an adjective and modifies the subject *we* of the main clause it introduces.)

IMPROVEMENT BY USE OF A GERUND PHRASE: *Losing the first game* made us vow to even the score the next day out. (A gerund phrase looks like a participial phrase. It starts with a gerund, also the *-ing* form of a verb—*losing*—except that a gerund or whole gerund phrase acts as a noun. Here it acts as the subject of a sentence whose verb is *made*.)

IMPROVEMENT BY USE OF A PREPOSITIONAL PHRASE: *After that first-game defeat*, we vowed to even the score the next day out. (A prepositional phrase, such as *before work, inside the CIA*, or *after our defeat*, consists of a preposition followed by a noun—*defeat*—and any modifiers of that noun—*that first-game*.)

IMPROVEMENT BY USE OF AN INFINITIVE PHRASE: *To lose the first game* was such a blow that we vowed to even the score the next day out. (An infinitive phrase starts with an infinitive—*to lose*—which is followed by a noun—*game*—and any modifiers of that noun—*the first*. The infinitive phrase in this suggested pattern acts as one whole noun, the subject of a sentence whose verb is *was*. Note that this sentence is also **complex,** consisting of a main clause beginning with *to lose* and a subordinate clause beginning with *that*.

For more information on sentence patterns, see *Subordination.* To learn how to knit sentences together to form a smooth paragraph, see *Paragraph* and *Transitions.* Here is a brief paragraph, modified from J. E. Oliver's *Perspectives on Applied Physical Geography,* that achieves sentence variety by employing subordination, coordination, and all of the phrase types discussed previously:

Making use of loud noises [gerund phrase] has been tried all over the world as a means *to change the weather.* [infinitive phrase] *In Europe, for example,* [prepositional phrases] people have tried *to prevent hailstorms,* [infinitive phrase] *for* [coordinating conjunction] hail has always caused considerable damage to vineyards. *To stop the hail from forming,* [infinitive phrase] farmers in northern Italy fired cannons at thunderclouds. Others felt *that they could stop storms* [relative clause] by *ringing church bells loudly.* [gerund phrase] Surprisingly, in some places *ringing bells* and *firing cannons* [gerund phrases] did seem to reduce the amount of crop damage by hail. This method became so popular *that it was finally outlawed.* [relative clause] Too many people were killed *by misfiring cannons* [prepositional phrase] and *by lightning* [prepositional phrase] *striking bell towers.* [participial phrase]

SENTENCE-LENGTH VARIETY

Good writers vary the pace and rhythm of their prose by mingling long, short, and medium-length sentences in any extended passage, as in the following paragraph (slightly modified from *Lunar Science: A Post-Apollo View*, by Stuart Ross Taylor):

119

The Apollo 11 landing on the moon took place on July 20, 1969, at 3:17:40 p.m., Eastern Standard Time, near the southern edge of Mare Tranquillitatis. [Medium-length sentence.] The site was named Tranquillity Base. [Short.] Astronauts Neil Armstrong and Edwin Aldrin collected 21.7 kilograms of samples in twenty minutes of hurried collecting toward the end of their two-hour sojourn (EVA, or extra-vehicular activity) on the lunar surface. [Medium-long.] These samples were received in the quarantine facilities of the Lunar Receiving Laboratory in Houston on July 25. [Short.] Four weeks of intensive examination began. [Short.] A team of scientific workers (the Lunar Sample Preliminary Examination Team, or LSPET, comprising eleven NASA scientists and fifteen other scientists from universities and government agencies) carried out preliminary geologic, geochemical, and biological examination of the samples, providing basic data for the Lunar Sample Analysis Planning Team (LSAPT). [Long.] Many of the first-order conclusions about the samples (such as their chemical uniqueness, their great age, and the absence of water, organic matter, and life) were established in this period. [Medium.]

Note the sequence of sentence-lengths in the previous paragraph: medium/short/medium-long/short/short/long/medium.

A. Practicing Sentence Variety

Convert the following pairs of simple sentences into each of the following:

(a) a compound sentence, using a comma and a coordinating conjunction (*and, but, for, nor, or, so, yet*). (Note that the use of *so* as a coordinating conjunction is frowned upon in formal English.)

(b) a complex sentence, using a subordinating conjunction (*after, although, because, if, since,* and so on) or a relative pronoun (*that, which,* and so on). (For a list of subordinators, see **Subordination.**)

(c) a single sentence in which you introduce *any* of the four following types of phrases: participial, gerund, prepositional, infinitive.

EXAMPLE: Much land in the United States is of little commercial value. It should be set aside for wildlife refuges.

ANSWER (a): Much land in the United States should be set aside for wildlife refuges, for it is of little commercial value. [a compound sentence]

ANSWER (b): Land in the United States that is of little commercial value should be set aside for wildlife refuges. [a complex sentence]

ANSWER (c): To make good use of much land in the United States bearing little commercial value, we should set it aside for wildlife refuges. [a sentence using both an infinitive *and* a participial phrase!]

1. Ron ran for a full hour. He did not become tired.

(a) _____

(b) _____

(c) _____

_____

2. Babe Ruth was superstitious. He kept his baseball cap in a cake box.

(a) _____

(b) _____

(c) _____

3. Tea is served as a beverage in China. It is also used there as a medicine.

(a) _____

(b) _____

(c) _____

_____

4. Television cameras use zoom lenses. These bring the action of sports events close to the viewer.

(a) _____

(b) _____

(c) _____

_____

5. Sarah turned the car around. She wanted to drive through the park.

(a) _____

(b) _____

(c) _____

_____

B. Sentence Variety in Paragraphs

The following paragraphs are made up of simple sentences only. In the space provided, rewrite each paragraph using at least *one example in each paragraph* of a simple sentence (S), a compound sentence (CP), a complex sentence (CX), and a sentence containing either a participial, a gerund, or an infinitive phrase (P). For the sake of coherence, use transitional words and phrases where necessary (see the lists under **Transitions**). In parentheses following each sentence, write the letter or letters that identify the sentence type.

EXAMPLE: Julius Caesar may not have been the most lovable character. He changed the course of history for the Western world. He demands our respect. He had brilliance on the battlefield. He had amazing charisma and power with words. His soldiers followed him with devotion. The devotion bordered on fanaticism. He led them from victory to victory. He had political greatness. He had generosity toward his defeated opponents. He became more than a ruler over the Roman people. They saw Caesar as a godlike figure. July is named in his honor. He was born in July.

REVISION: Julius Caesar may not have been the most lovable character, but he changed the course of history in the Western world. (CP) Demanding our respect for his brilliance on the battlefield, he also had an amazing charisma and power with words. (P) His soldiers followed him with a devotion that bordered on fanaticism as he led them from victory to victory. (CX) He had political greatness that expressed itself in his generosity toward his defeated opponents. (CX) He became more than a ruler over his people, for the Romans saw Caesar as a godlike figure. (CP) July, his birthmonth, is named in his honor. (S)

● 1.   The only intelligent life in the universe exists on our planet, Earth. This long-standing belief is gradually disappearing. Some scientists estimate the existence of one million advanced civilizations. This estimate is for the Milky Way galaxy alone. Many prominent scientists are attempting to contact these possible civilizations. They are well aware of the risks of such contact. In all probability, the benefits would outweigh the risks. Contact with alien civilizations could result in advancements in every sphere of science and technology. Scientists are still wary, however. They might encounter an unfriendly form of alien life. Their emphasis is on receiving possible signals rather than establishing two-way communication.

123

Your revision:

_____

_____

_____

_____

_____

_____

_____

_____

_____

_____

2.   Monsters have been with us since the beginning of time. They range from legendary dragons to werewolves and vampires. Some are imaginary. Many people firmly believe in the existence of one—the Loch Ness Monster. Documentation supports its existence. Loch Ness is a 14,000-acre lake in Scotland. The Loch Ness Monster is nicknamed Nessie. It was first sighted in 565 A.D. It is still seen at regular intervals. Observers estimate its dimensions. It ranges from twenty to forty feet in length. Submarine exploration has proven useless. The waters of Loch Ness are too murky. There have been many photographs and motion pictures of what is believed to be Nessie. In 1968 Professor D. G. Tucker of Birmingham University used a digital sonar at Loch Ness. His readout showed the presence of at least *two* very large animals. This finding is not surprising. A breeding population would be needed. The lake became landlocked 6,500 years ago!

Your revision:

_____

_____

_____

_____

_____

_____

_____

_____

_____

_____

C. Varying the Lengths of Sentences

Using one of the following topics, construct an interesting paragraph of at least five sentences in which you consciously vary your sentence *lengths.* Leave a space after each sentence to label it as "(Short)," "(Medium)," or "(Long)."

TOPICS:

1. My conflict over a choice of major (or profession)

2. Is love more important than money?

3. My honest opinion about drugs

4. The quality of current television entertainment

5. A vivid dream

6. An important interest (or hobby) of mine

After finishing your paragraph, reread it to determine how many different types of *structure* you have employed (simple, compound, and complex sentences; participial, gerund, prepositional, and infinitive phrases). If you do not find *at least four* different structures, rewrite the paragraph until you do.

WORDINESS——————————————wdy

Get rid of unnecessary and repetitious wording. Whenever possible, condense. Do not pad your sentences with "deadwood"—words or phrases that add nothing to the meaning.

PADDED: In my own personal opinion, attendance at this meeting should be mandatory.

REVISED: In my opinion, attendance at this meeting should be mandatory.

PADDED: Although Hank did not like the subject area of mathematics, he did well on the final exam.

REVISED: Although Hank did not like mathematics, he did well on the final exam.

PADDED: Because of the fact that the coastline had been invaded by jellyfish, the lifeguard posted the "no swimming" sign.

REVISED: Because the coastline had been invaded by jellyfish, the lifeguard posted the "no swimming" sign.

1. Avoid the unnecessary repetition of words and ideas:

REPETITIOUS: The play *The Glass Menagerie,* by Tennessee Williams, is a play about hopes and dreams.

REVISED: *The Glass Menagerie,* by Tennessee Williams, is a play about hopes and dreams.

REPETITIOUS: Driving on icy roads can be extremely hazardous and dangerous.

REVISED: Driving on icy roads can be extremely dangerous.

2. Where possible, use short, direct grammatical constructions:

LONG: I was responsible for overall maintenance, but it was Henry who did most of the repair jobs.

SHORTER: I was responsible for overall maintenance, but Henry did most of the repair jobs.

INDIRECT: The plants were watered by Katrina.

DIRECT: Katrina watered the plants. (Use the active voice instead of the passive. See *Passive Voice.*)

● **A. Rewriting Sentences to Eliminate Wordiness**

EXAMPLE: On the subject of evolution, Dr. Richard Leakey is a known expert.
REVISED: Dr. Richard Leakey is an expert on evolution.

1. The tour guide, who was friendly in manner, showed us many parts of Morocco which were uniquely unusual.

_____

_____

2. Jim was issued a ticket because of the fact that he zipped past a traffic light when it was red in color.

_____

_____

3. The nature of that drastic emergency situation called for decisive action of a military nature.

_____

_____

4. Marlene suggested the idea of going to Lake George and then the conception of going to Montreal for the mid-term break.

_____

_____

5. Cynthia Schneider, film editor for the film *Breaking Away,* did an excellent and superlative job editing the Cinzano truck scene in the film *Breaking Away.*

_____

_____

B. Rewriting a Paragraph to Eliminate Wordiness

Because of the fact that video games have become so very popular in our modern society today, there has been much controversy as to their effect upon society and our culture. Many parents, teachers, educators, physicians, and doctors have become concerned about the possible bad effects and hazardous consequences that these games might have upon children of this generation. In their personal opinion, they feel that video games can become addictive like drugs or gambling. They think that children who play these various and sundry video games can become obsessed with a desire to win. Also, many people are of the opinion that these video games encourage violence because of the fact that so many of these games are based upon themes of war and battle. However, other people from the other side of the controversy are of a different point of view. These people are of the opinion that playing video games can be beneficial to children playing them. For example, they feel that playing these video games can develop a child's hand-eye coordination. Also, many people think playing video games helps to develop necessary skills for competing in today's competitive world. Whichever side is of the right opinion, video games will be staying with our modern society for a long while yet.

Your revision:

_____

_____

_____

_____

_____

_____

_____

_____

Review Exercise: Choppy Sentences

Combine each group of sentences into one sentence, eliminating choppiness. To review methods for achieving smooth sentence structure, see the headnotes in this book for **Choppy Sentences, Subordination, Transitions,** and **Variety in Sentence Patterns.**

EXAMPLE: Prince Edward's Island is a Canadian province. It is situated in the Gulf of St. Lawrence. Prince Edward's Island is the only Canadian province located off the mainland.

REVISION: Prince Edward's Island, a Canadian province in the Gulf of St. Lawrence, is the only Canadian province located off the mainland.

1. Prince Edward's Island was named in honor of British King George III's son. His name was Prince Edward.

_____

_____

2. It is known by natives as "the Island." It is also known as "P.E.I." It is a scenic tourist attraction.

_____

_____

3. It is Canada's smallest province. It is thickly populated.

_____

_____

4. Charlottetown is the capital of Prince Edward's Island. It is the island's only city.

_____

_____

5. P.E.I. is covered by fertile red soil. It is surrounded by excellent fishing waters. The island is famous for its agriculture and fishing industries.

_____

_____

6. Its chief crop is potatoes. P.E.I. exports thousands of bushels of potatoes each year.

_____

_____

7. It is best known for its tourism trade. The beaches are long and sandy. The beach sand is either pure white or ruddy red.

_____

_____

8. Charlottetown offers horse races. These occur only during the summer months. Horse racing is an enjoyable pastime.

_____

_____

9. The island has several golf courses. It offers streams for fishing. It has waterways for sailing.

_____

_____

10. The climate is temperate. The warm ocean currents make P.E.I.'s seashore enjoyable during the summer months. It is an attractive vacation spot.

_____

_____

Review Exercise: Commas

Correct all comma errors in the following sentences. Insert missing commas. Circle commas that should be omitted.

EXAMPLE: Although most people do not consider procrastination a serious problem, its effects may be crippling.

1. Because prolonged procrastination can be destructive more and more people are seeking professional help to combat this problem.

2. In so many cases of prolonged stubborn procrastination people have lost their jobs and even destroyed family relationships.

3. Because of sheer procrastination, people dawdle endlessly over doctoral dissertations or go to jail for income tax evasion.

4. The American procrastinator has a particularly hard time because America an extremely fast-paced country places many competitive demands on people.

5. Little research has been done on this subject because procrastination has always been a source of humor and has never been taken seriously.

6. However in recent years psychologists and behavioral scientists have started to investigate the hidden causes of procrastination.

7. Contrary to popular belief procrastinators are not all lazy.

8. Dr. Lenora M. Yuen a psychologist at the University of California says "If you scratch a procrastinator, you'll find a workaholic."

9. Among the several causes of procrastination are low self-esteem fear of rejection and internal conflict.

10. The problem does not stem simply from the avoidance of unpleasant tasks, that can always be done later.

11. One latent reason for procrastination is the fear of failure and a related reason is perfectionism.

12. Many procrastinators delay because they are afraid, of not making the grade, and of being rejected.

13. Perfectionist-procrastinators often need to set themselves strict deadlines, to avoid revising and revamping forever.

14. Another reason for procrastination one not as common as fear of failure is a resistance to authority.

15. People subject to this type of procrastination are reluctant to voice hostile feelings openly but they get revenge by being late.

16. Still other procrastinators fear success, and are often hesitant to succeed at the expense of others' happiness.

17. This problem is particularly true among working women, who have husbands and families.

18. Students, writers professors and lawyers people who must set their own schedules, are all prime candidates for procrastinating.

19. Not all procrastination however is work-related.

20. People, who are never late for work, can often neglect household chores for weeks.

Review Exercise: Commas and Semicolons

Correct all comma and semicolon errors in the following sentences. Insert missing commas or semicolons. Circle commas or semicolons that should be dropped. If a comma should replace a semicolon, or vice versa, circle the error and place the correct mark beneath it.

EXAMPLE: Although Wales has been under British rule for hundreds of years,the Welsh people maintain a cultural heritage of their own.

1. Long before Anglo-Saxon or Norman rule, the people of Wales were speaking an offshoot of the Celtic language, called Welsh, however today only twenty percent of the Welsh population speaks the language.

2. Welsh which was once spoken at King Arthur's legendary court lost popularity during Britain's Industrial Revolution.

3. However efforts have been made in recent years to restore the Welsh language to its original prominence and in 1982 the British government supported the development of the Welsh-language television channel.

4. Although a Welsh person might speak English the accent is often so thick that it is indecipherable to the American ear.

5. Nowadays it is not uncommon to see bilingual, road signs and; in some cases overly enthusiastic Welsh nationalists have taken to spray-painting Welsh words over English ones.

6. Language however, is not the only part of Welsh culture Wales is also a land of ancient castles, stone fortresses, and pastoral beauty.

7. At a spring festival called the Eisteddfod the Welsh remember the ancient Druids a race that once inhabited the land.

8. The festival somewhat resembles May Day; and is celebrated with festive song and dance.

9. Although Dylan Thomas, a poet and native of south Wales did not write in Welsh his writing reflects a deep regard for the heritage.

10. All of its tradition and heritage makes Wales popular with tourists; who enjoy visiting the Gower Peninsula, a favorite seashore spot, Laugharne, the home of Dylan Thomas, and Snowdonia National Park, a camping ground.

Review Exercise: Fragments, Run-Ons, and Comma Splices

Revise each of the following sentences to eliminate fragment, run-on, and comma-splice errors. You may need to add, or leave out, words or punctuation marks.

EXAMPLE: George Gershwin was born into a Russian immigrant home. And, raised in Brooklyn, New York.

REVISION: George Gershwin was born into a Russian immigrant home and was raised in Brooklyn, New York.

1. George Gershwin was an American composer who lived from 1898 to 1937, He is famous for popular songs, musicals, and symphonies.

   _____

   _____

2. His first successful composition was "Swanee," A song which Al Jolson performed and made a hit.

   _____

   _____

3. He started to write popular songs at age fifteen, he also studied music and orchestration his entire life.

   _____

   _____

4. Gershwin had two ambitions. To compose successful popular pieces and to live up to the reputations of the great masters.

   _____

   _____

5. Gershwin became most famous in the 1920s for his Broadway musical comedies, for example, he wrote *Lady Be Good* (1924) and *Funny Face* (1927).

   _____

   _____

6. In 1930 Gershwin wrote *Girl Crazy* at this point he turned to political satire and wrote the musical comedy *Strike Up the Band* (1930).

_____

_____

7. In 1931 Gershwin wrote another political musical comedy called *Of Thee I Sing,* this was a spoof on presidential elections.

_____

_____

8. *Of Thee I Sing* was very well received. And the first musical to receive a Pulitzer prize.

_____

_____

9. Gershwin's works include tunes still popular today for example, he wrote "I Got Rhythm" and "Embraceable You."

_____

_____

10. Gershwin's brother, Ira, wrote the lyrics for most of the songs. All of them extremely memorable.

_____

_____

Review Exercise: Modifiers

In the space beside each sentence, indicate if the sentence contains a *dangling* or a *misplaced* modifier by writing "D" or "M." Write "C" if the sentence is correct as it stands. In the space below each sentence, write a revised version of each incorrect one.

EXAMPLE: __D__ Arriving at the airport in a panic, my plane had already taken off.

REVISION: Arriving at the airport in a panic, I found out that my plane had already taken off.

_____ 1. While champing on the bit, the jockey led the race horse to the starting gate.

_____

_____

_____ 2. I watched the Rose Parade in my car.

_____

_____

_____ 3. Dave bought a car from someone that had an oil leak.

_____

_____

_____ 4. Reading books occasionally is good for the soul.

_____

_____

_____ 5. At the age of ten, Martha's parents were divorced.

_____

_____

_____ 6. While using a twenty-pound test line, the huge marlin easily got away.

_____

_____

_____ 7. Does driving at night sometimes cause blurred vision?

_____

_____

_____ 8. After playing football, my uniform needs to be patched.

_____

_____

_____ 9. Because of the power failure, New York City was without lights for two days.

_____

_____

_____ 10. Students expecting a rise in tuition soon might be surprised.

_____

_____

Review Exercise: Pronouns

Revise the following passages, making any changes necessary to eliminate pronoun problems in agreement, case, reference, and shifts in point of view.

EXAMPLE: In 1980, Japan's auto production surpassed that of the United States. This helps to explain the steadily rising unemployment figures in Detroit.

REVISION: In 1980, Japan's auto production surpassed that of the United States. This increase helps to explain the steadily rising unemployment figures in Detroit. (Unclear reference of the pronoun *this.*)

1. What made the Japanese car particularly attractive to Americans was their high gas-mileage ratings.

_____

_____

2. OPEC's skyrocketing oil prices forced citizens like you and I to buy more and more economical and compact cars.

_____

_____

3. The increase in gas prices in 1973 helped companies like Datsun and Subaru to sell its cars.

_____

_____

4. One began to realize that the Japanese cars were much better on mileage than our own "gas guzzlers."

_____

_____

5. At one time, us Americans viewed the label "made in Japan" as a sign of shoddy workmanship.

_____

_____

140

6. Many of us now perceive Japanese technology as superior to our own, which is destructive to the morale of the American business community.

_____

_____

7. The craftsmanship of American auto workers seems to have dropped to their lowest point in many years.

_____

_____

8. In 1977 alone, the countless deficiencies in American vehicles caused them to recall more than were produced.

_____

_____

9. The American labor force was criticized for being inefficient, but they carried on in the same way.

_____

_____

10. Although they were not discovered by American businessmen until the early eighties, the secret of Japan's marketing successes proved very revealing.

_____

_____

11. For years the American businessman believed that his marketing techniques were the best, but they were soon disabused of this notion.

_____

_____

12. When American business executives took a stroll through a Japanese auto plant, we experienced a shocking revelation.

_____

_____

13. If one walks past a Japanese assembly line, you will notice that all movement is brisk and efficient.

_____

_____

14. It said in a *National Geographic* article that all new employees at Japanese auto plants receive weeks of instruction in company history and policy.

_____

_____

15. Excellent labor-management relations at Japanese motor companies help to explain its success, but it is only a part of the explanation.

_____

_____

16. Neither labor nor management is seen as more important, which furnishes a clue to their high morale.

_____

_____

17. At one Japanese plant, the number of steps in a particular operation of theirs was cut in half because of a worker's suggestion.

_____

_____

18. Everyone at Japanese plants know they play an important role in production.

_____

_____

19. A Japanese auto worker is content to receive lower pay than his or her American counterpart because he or she gets extraordinary fringe benefits.

_____

_____

20. The Japanese worker is bound closely to the company by reason of the many benefits, such as subsidized housing and free vacations, of which they are assured.

_____

_____

ANSWER KEY

Note to the Student: It is important to remember that many of the exercises in this book allow for more than just one correct answer. The answers to such exercises represent only one *possibility,* not the *only* possible answer, and not necessarily the best answer. The headnotes before each exercise indicate the degree of flexibility you have in composing answers.

Adjective
1. terrible   2. worst   3. good   4. omit "more"   5. C   6. well   7. bad
8. disturbing   9. good   10. omit "more"

Adverb
1. mercilessly   2. very long   3. awfully   4. comparatively   5. exhausted
6. typical   7. even worse than   8. wonderfully   9. C   10. devices certainly began

Agreement
A. ss = simple subject; v = verb; the correct form of the verb or the letter "C" (for *correct*) is given in parentheses.

1. ss = deer; v = eat(eats)/ ss = food; v = is(C)
2. ss = honeysuckle, clover, soybeans, and . . . crab-apple; v = is(are)/ ss = deer;
   v = enjoys(C)
3. ss = one; v = are(is)
4. ss = deer; v = die(C)/ ss = storms; v = get(C)/ ss = they; v = are(C)
5. ss = civilization; v = causes(C)/ ss = overfeeding and . . . land; v = leads(lead)
6. ss = invasion; v come(comes)
7. ss = hunters; v takes(take)
8. ss = sense; v = are(is)
9. ss = set; v = promote(promotes)
10. ss = hunger, v = keep(keeps)

Apostrophe
1. Simpson's/didn't/weeks'/sister's/summer's
2. guests/mayor's/daughters'/VIPs or VIP's
3. Club's/Dad's/sets/novels/weren't
4. hospital's/R.N.'s/years'/disputes
5. 1600s or 1600's/1930s/companies'/productions/Miller's/Steinbeck's

Capitalization
1. Cold War/War II   2. New York/Museum of Natural History   3. Roman/B.C.
4. How/history   5. south/winter   6. Hitchcock/*North by Northwest*   7. Museum/
Sunday   8. Carthaginian/Hannibal/Rome   9. graduate mathematics   10. Civil War/
Europe   11. Beatles/Maharishi/Indian guru   12. Fourth/truck/Cape   13. history
14. vacuum cleaner   15. microchip industry/Japanese   16. terrestrials/Newtonian
17. fall   18. Building   19. *to*/Indian/British   20. *yuppie*/young urban professional

144

Case

A. 1. ~~You~~ Your   2. ~~Her~~ She   3. C   4. ~~her~~ she   5. ~~me~~ I   6. C   7. ~~who~~ whom
8. ~~Whom~~ Who   9. ~~Whoever~~ Whomever   10. ~~I~~ Me

C. 1. Whose   2. whose   3. It's   4. whose   5. its   6. it's   7. who's   8. whose   9. it's
10. its

Coherence

A. The following answer key gives the word or phrase that acts as a linking device
and then identifies it with a bracketed number:

1. They [3]/fear that scientists [2]   2. On the other hand [1]/animal/such test-
tube creatures[2]   3. Instead[1]/ they [3]/ material [2]/ living [2]   4. for example [1]/
gene [2]   5. this [4]/ goal [2]/ however [1]   6. such [3]/ procedures [2]/ these[4]/
experimenters [2]

Colon

1. life:anxiety   2. except fear   3. prized:portability   4. on widespread   5. husbandry," which   6. say:"Even   7. C   8. is a   9. reading: science   10. mix: drinking

Comma

A. 1. symbols, for   2. anyone, and   3. cards, but   4. $27,000, yet   5. cards, so   6. C
7. cards, and   8. future, for   9. electronically, for   10. future, but

C. 1. something,   2. obsessive,   3. C   4. fact,   5. *engrams,*   6. ago Descartes
7. models,   8. technology,   9. course,   10. C

D. 1. ages, . . . present,   2. philosophers, . . . inhabited,   3. Plutarch, . . . *Moon,*   4. C
5. C   6. Lucretius, . . . worlds,   7. thinkers, . . . opposed,   8. Church, . . . omnipotence,
9. grounds, however,   10. evidence, of course,

F. 1. scorn, impatience, sarcasm,   2. tyrants, . . . prisons,   3. teachers, . . . patience,
4. hardware, . . . software,   5. future, . . . education,   6. drills, practice exercises,/facts,
skills,   7. method, the tutorial method,   8. life, limb,   9. subjects, . . . materials,
10. textbooks, audio lectures, film loops, T.V. shows,

Comma Splice/Run-On

The following revisions indicate only *some* of the ways in which these sentences can
be corrected:

1. crime because the/RO   2. million, but his/CS   3. C   4. criminals. Auditing/RO
5. loss; however,/CS   6. trail"; invoices/RO   7. exist; for/CS   8. prosecution; in/RO
9. publicity. After/CS   10. difficult. The/CS

Comparison

1. any *other* existing   2. than *in* the   3. than *developments in* biology   4. than *that of*
Mars   5. as important *as*   6. than *that of* any   7. you *do.*   8. as famous *as*   9. as *those
of* astronomers   10. than *a trip to* our

Emphasis

A.

1. Hindus venerate cows because the cow is the symbol of everything that is alive.
2. India's cows wander through the streets, browse off market stalls, break into private gardens, and defecate all over the sidewalks.
3. In Madras the police nurse stray cattle that are ill back to health by letting them graze on small fields adjacent to the station house.
4. Hindu farmers regard their cows as members of the family, adorn them with garlands and tassels, and pray for them when they get sick.
5. Cows are important to the Indian ecosystem in ways, however, that are easily overlooked or demeaned by observers from industrialized countries.
6. The economic functions of the zebu cow include a marginal amount of milk production, the provision of dung used for fertilizer and cooking fuel, and the breeding of the indispensable male traction animals.

Fragmentary Sentence

B. There are many ways to correct fragments other than the following:

1. SC/ There is a difference between science and technology.
2. C
3. A/ It is fascinating to read about cosmology, the study of the universe's structure.
4. P/ Cosmogony is the study of the universe's origin.
5. SC/ Although the early philosophers knew nothing of the physical laws that govern matter, Lucretius arrived intuitively at a sort of atomic theory.
6. P/ An example of an early cosmogony is a tradition from India that pictures the universe as a giant egg.
7. P/ Traveling at the speed of light is considered impossible, according to present-day physicists.
8. C
9. A/ The word *quasar* is an acronym for *qua*si-*stellar* radio source.
10. P/ The plausible idea that many stars should have planets is based on our current knowledge of star-formation.

Italics

Mozambique/ the *New Yorker*/ the *Atlantic Monthly*/ the *London Times*/ the *Allgemeine Zeitung*/*Le Figaro*/*La Bohème*/*The Thinker*/*Old Goriot*/*The Red and the Black*/*King Kong*/*Casablanca*/*Titanic*/*Jurassic Park*/ spelled *Europe* without the first *E*/ words like *and* and *the*/ with *stop*/*Mozambique*/*de luxe*

Paragraph

A. I. Sentences (4) and (6) disrupt *unity;* they do not develop the topic—the film's effect on popularizing disco.

II. Sentence (4) disrupts *coherence;* either drop the sentence or let the paragraph begin with it. Sentence (7) disrupts *unity;* it does not develop the topic—specifically, the technique of acupuncture.

III. Sentences (4) and (5) disrupt *unity;* they do not develop the topic—what you can learn from listening to professional writers.

146

Parallelism

A.

1. For the aspiring writer, the accumulation of rejection slips is a rite of passage, a test of endurance, and a concrete proof that one is, after all, a writer.

2. The most important lesson of literature is that we are not alone in suffering the agonies of childhood, adolescence, and adulthood.

3. If you want to be a good writer, you have to be a good listener and a good reader.

4. If you want to write effectively, keep your main point in mind, don't stray too far from it without good reason, and develop it in convincing detail.

5. James Dickey was a poet, a novelist, and a literary critic.

Pronoun Reference

Many correct answers are possible.

1. Our continuing interest in UFOs is maintained by new books on these alien visitors and is stoked by our love of the exotic. *This double appeal to emotion* is enough to inspire uncritical belief in many people.

2. William's extra-terrestrial captor told him that he was not *a very healthy earthling.*

3. The alien would never be able to get home, *a conclusion* which saddened everyone who watched the film.

4. As I saw the monster heading toward my unsuspecting son, I shouted at *the boy* as loudly as I could.

5. John wondered whether the invading Arcturan had implanted in Peter an intelligence as great as *the monster's own.*

6. The starving astronauts roasted and devoured the alien creature, *a feast* which resulted in their being charged with murder.

7. When the great-eyed octopod whipped a tentacle out for my gun, I hurled *the weapon* spinning away into space.

8. In the early days of science fiction, it was difficult for female writers to get published in the genre. *This prejudice* prompted many women writers to use male pen names.

9. Until recently, sexism reigned supreme in the science-fiction magazine market. An article on *this sexist bias* appeared in last week's *Atlantic Monthly.*

10. The bulk of science fiction still neglects character development in favor of plot, *an imbalance* which renders the genre suspect in the eyes of serious readers of literature.

Quotation Marks

1. "Most men," Thoreau says, "are . . . them."

2. "Men . . . mistake," Thoreau says. "They . . . corrupt."

3. Thoreau claims, "The . . . desperation"; . . .

4. asked, "What . . . to?"

5. said, "Cast . . . items"?

6. poem "The Coming . . . Time," Sheila read the article "Yeats's View of Aging in 'The Coming . . . Time.' "

7. "shine"

8. I . . . Hand" was . . .

9. "cinch"

10. "To His Coy Mistress" and "A Valediction: Forbidding Mourning."

Semicolon

A. 1. time; they   2. changing, that   3. painting but [*or*] painting, but it   4. music; however   5. perspective; the/harmony; and

Shift in Point of View

B.

1. Some students read their textbook assignments passively, whereas others make marginal comments liberally in response to particularly challenging material.

2. In ancient India, a famous yellow pigment was made from the urine of specially fed cows, but the same color can now be manufactured without the need for animal intervention.

3. Although we would like one day to be able to exceed the speed of light, we will most probably never accomplish such a feat.

4. We spent three hours cooking dinner, and then we ate it in fifteen minutes.

5. You should first mow the lawn, and then you should repair the fence.

Subordination

A. Many correct answers are possible.

1. When his parachute opened, the sky diver knew he was saved.

2. Taking careful aim, he squeezed the trigger slowly.

3. Hesitating, he finally plunked down his money on the long shot.

4. She was elected company president because she was the most talented of all the managers.

5. Martha was so bright that she had to drop her French class, which dragged on too slowly to suit her.

6. She unhappily had to choose between partying and studying.

7. Dora is a computer whiz, whereas her brother John can play five musical instruments.

8. Taking a chance, she arrived at the airport just in time.

9. Tired and hungry, we got home just before dark.

10. She zipped confidently through the exam in only half an hour.

Transitions

Many correct answers are possible.

1. Nevertheless,   2. As a result,   3. In fact,   4. , however,   5. In spite of that, 6. Consequently,   7. On the other hand,   8. indeed   9. , for example,   10. Finally,

Variety in Sentence Patterns

B. A sample answer is given for paragraph 1 only:

1. The long-standing belief that the only intelligent life in the universe exists on our plant, Earth, is gradually disappearing. (CX) Some scientists estimate the existence of one million advanced civilizations in the Milky Way galaxy alone. (S) Although they are well aware of the risks, many prominent scientists are attempting to contact these civilizations. (CX) In all probability, the benefits would greatly outweigh the risks, and contact with alien civilizations could result in advancements in every sphere of science and technology. (CP) Scientists are still wary, however. (S) Fearing an encounter with an unfriendly form of life, their emphasis is only on receiving possible signals rather than establishing two-way communication. (P)

Wordiness

A.

1. The friendly tour guide showed us many unusual parts of Morocco.
2. Jim was issued a traffic ticket because he zipped past a red light.
3. The emergency called for decisive military action.
4. Marlene suggested going to Lake George and then to Montreal for the mid-term break.
5. Cynthia Schneider, film editor for *Breaking Away,* did an excellent job with the Cinzano truck scene.